Singapore Mutiny

Singapore Mutiny

A colonial couple's stirring account
of combat and survival
in the 1915 Singapore Mutiny

EDWIN A. BROWN
MARY BROWN

monsoon

monsoonbooks

Published in 2015
by Monsoon Books Pte Ltd
www.monsoonbooks.com.sg

Editorial / Sales:
No.1 Duke of Windsor Suite, Burrough Court,
Burrough on the Hill, Leics. LE14 2QS, UK

Registered office:
150 Orchard Road #07-02, Singapore 238841

First edition.

ISBN (paperback): 978-981-4625-05-0
ISBN (ebook): 978-981-4625-06-7

Cover design by Cover Kitchen.
All cover and inside photographs©Celia Ferguson, except 'Mutineers
face the firing squad'©Whitaker Family (IWM).
Handwritten account transcribed by Michael Tatham.

Printed in USA
17 16 15   1 2 3 4 5

To Barbara Mary Brown
with love from
Mummy and Daddy

in remembrance of a very stirring
and exciting period of our lives

Foreword

Brian P. Farrell

The subtitle captures the memoir. *A colonial couple's stirring account of combat and survival in the 1915 Singapore Mutiny*, is just what it promises to be, with a little bit extra. The issue is perspective. The Great War experience in Singapore will always be deeply overshadowed by the far more intense impact a Second World War had on the island and its residents. Compared side by side, it really looks as if very little happened on and around the island from 1914-1918. This however is to measure by one, admittedly a big one, index of conflict: military operations and casualties. Singapore was conquered and occupied in 1942. Only two military operations of any note took place anywhere near the island the first time around, both were short lived episodes, and as it turns out both were connected.

The Second World War experience produced an ongoing flood of personal memoirs and eyewitness accounts. The Great War episodes generated no more than a trickle. All the more important then, when another drip comes out of the pipe, because the Singapore Great War experience was itself consequential, dramatic, and produced lasting repercussions rippling beyond the island – scaled down, of course. In place of Force Z and the end of the era of the battleship there was the rampage of the German cruiser *Emden*, her destruction in November 1914, and the imprisonment of her survivors on Dempsey Hill, at Tanglin Barracks. In place of huge numbers of casualties from enemy bombing and shelling, there was the return to Europe of a high percentage of the small European community in Singapore, to fight for King, Country and Empire, and the predictably high percentage of casualties from that group. And in place of enemy conquest and occupation there was a Mutiny – a short, but sharp, violent, controversial, and consequential upheaval from within – an episode, but one that exposed the very fault lines of multi-racial Empire. Edwin A. Brown, already a well-established businessman and Volunteer officer, lived on to become a major figure in Singapore life – and to be caught up in the Second and far Greater World War. But in February 1915 he and his young family, living comfortably in one of the splendid white and black bungalows in the European residential district of Tanglin, regarded then as an 'outlying district', found themselves caught up in the very heart of the turmoil that erupted on the afternoon of

Monday 15 February, the second day of the Chinese New Year holiday, when half of the 5th Light Infantry 'came out'.

Brown and his wife Mary wrote this memoir in 1925, for their daughter Barbara, who was three years old when the Sepoy Mutiny took place. This is the first of four features that give this account greater value; rather than being subjected to any post-Second World War sanitization of attitude, language, or memory, the Browns recall their experience within the world view that still prevailed in a British Empire that still stood very tall, East of Suez, in a truly British world. The Browns had a Chinese 'boy', who Edwin at least refers to by name, a Malay syce, an Amah to nurse the baby, always capitalized, never named. They lived a life of imperial comfort and privilege. Mutineers were 'devils' and when they 'came out' no European needed any further explanation regarding the threat. The Raffles Hotel instinctively appeared as a safe refuge to those in 'outlying districts', despite the fact it had no special protection from any attack. When that fact became obvious, the dire threat the 'devils' posed to European women, referred to only in guarded, indirect language, compelled a retreat to the greater safety of ships anchored offshore. Islands of refuge, on and off shore, in alien surroundings? The Brown memoir captures, vividly, not only the European mood of the time and place, but adds detailed value to this by combining both his and her accounts, in separate chapters, of their different experiences. Both Browns have an eye for character, detail, and mood. And both refer to central themes that not only shaped this event but also connected it to wider historical forces: subversion and sedition; colonial complacency; class and race; power and security.

The Browns only hint at one of the wider and more interesting political dynamics that probably made some difference to the February 1915 mutiny: violent Indian nationalism in general, and the Ghadr movement in particular. Ghadr, Urdu for 'rebellion,' was founded in North America by Punjabi expatriates who hoped to spark the Indian Army to lead what would become a national uprising, to drive the British out of India. The entry of Ottoman Turkey into the war on the side of the Central Powers complicated the problem. Sultan Mehmed V had a fatwa, or religious ruling of instruction, issued, calling on all Muslims to rise up against the British Empire, and the German secret service worked to stoke these flames of religious rebellion inside the huge Muslim communities living under British rule. Both these wider waves of turbulence came into Singapore and had some effect on the all-Muslim rank and file of the 5th Light. British security forces dealt very effectively with these threats, aborting or quickly suppressing all Ghadr efforts to 'bring out' the Army in India. But one of the few possible objectives that made any sense for the mutiny that did break out, within the 5th Light in Singapore, was the idea that the mutineers could overwhelm the weak defence of the colony, free the German prisoners of war, many of them sailors and naval officers, and with their help commandeer a ship and make for India. They certainly seem to have at least tried to do some such thing. A full century of enquiry suggests that neither the Ghadr nor the Germans actually provoked the Singapore Mutiny, but both had some influence on those troops of the Rajput wing of the battalion who did take up arms. Edwin Brown certainly discussed the widespread belief on the ground, at the time, that the Germans were somehow complicit. Tellingly, he goes out of his way to praise them, incorrectly, for refusing 'to a man' to help the mutineers in any way – a penetrating insight into a prevailing pan-European imperial worldview in Asia.

Both Browns testify vividly as to how weak the defences of Singapore were in mid-February 1915, despite the fact that the only trained regular infantry battalion in the garrison, the 5th Light, was already seen as unreliable and uneasy. Chance naturally played a large role in the drama that ensued, well captured in both accounts by memories narrow misses with rampaging mutineers, comments on the importance of action that was not only bold but more important timely, and above all by the strain on the nerves caused by having to work with so little solid information. One theme runs through the story of the mutiny from the official court and report of enquiry produced during the war to the most recent studies published by scholars: leadership.

Angry and frightened residents of Singapore denounced the official conclusions at the time for placing the greatest weight of blame for the uprising on poor leadership within the battalion, from the commanding officer on down. This was dismissed as covering up wider problems. Many subsequent accounts paid some attention to this theme, for similar reasons. But criticism and revision never really dispelled the original conclusion. The Brown memoir provides some pretty compelling testimony in its support. Edwin spent most of the first phase of the mutiny at or near the sharp end of the fighting. His account vividly describes how improvised the garrisons response had to be, how untrained most 'loyal' volunteers were, and by some direct references develops a crucial point: whatever else they were, the mutineers were trained regular soldiers who knew how to use their weapons and had some understanding of field-craft. This made them, in his view, a very serious threat considering the motley array that at first stood between them and the city. Leadership then intersected with another crucial factor, time, to decisively shape the event. A bold decision by the naval commander of the small squadron in the harbor to improvise a shore party and immediately commit it to battle, to try to prevent the mutineers from overwhelming the docks on the run, paid a crucial dividend when skirmishes between that shore party and a group of mutineers apparently killed one of the ringleaders of the uprising, a senior non-commissioned officer who played a major role in organizing the initial movement. The mutineers went on to waste something no army can ever regain, time, by dithering in indecision after the lukewarm reception they received from the German prisoners of war – and above all by putting the house of their commanding officer under siege, then allowing this to drag on all night, rather than either taking it by storm or smoking him out. Brown's account makes it crystal clear that for that all-important first afternoon and evening the scratch forces left to defend Singapore could not have withstood an organized and determined advance to a purpose by more than 400 heavily armed regular infantry. No such advance was made. Crowning the point, Brown makes a persuasive case that the bold call by Colonel C.W. Brownlow, a vastly experienced regular artillery officer, to attack the mutineers holding their barracks and besieging their commanding officer, rather than fall back onto defensive positions, was an inspired and decisive command decision. Outnumbered and outgunned, and at some cost, the boldness of the attack carried the day

– the difference being the clear exercise of command to a purpose on the one side, the disarray and dithering on the other. This suggests that the role of the Allied reinforcements which arrived over the next few days was to mop up, not break, the uprising. Brown makes a real contribution here.

Nevertheless, the most important reason why this memoir will take a place on the list of required reading for this event in Singapore and British Empire history is the sense of time, place and people that it evokes so well. The juxtaposition of the his and her accounts and experiences nicely adds width to the witness they bear on the event as a whole. The most fascinating point of intersection must be the initial dash to the Raffles Hotel. In the midst of that worst colonial nightmare East of Suez, with native troops 'out' and no European regulars close by to respond, both Browns took it for granted that safety and security could be found, at least at first, in the warm embrace of the Hotel. That assumption crumbles immediately under scrutiny. Had the mutineers determined from the start that their first move was to make an all-out organized assault on the Hotel, what could have stopped them? The imposing, but unarmed, Sikh doormen? Clarity soon prevailed, leading to the further dash to the ships. But there was no assault, and the entire European community had that same instinctive reaction as to where to make the first dash for refuge. The irony is that these two very different groups probably behaved as they did for the same reason: surely no one could even imagine mutineers attacking the Hotel, willfully capitalized. The Browns add a colourful first hand account to what we already know was the cardinal fact of the Singapore Mutiny of 1915: that such an uprising could ever have happened at all.

Professor Brian P. Farrell
Department of History
National University of Singapore

Foreword

Nigel Barley

On February 16th 1915, the *Straits Times* appeared on the streets of Singapore in an abbreviated form. Its editorial explained, 'Circumstances, which we shall have an opportunity of explaining at greater length in due course have made us decide to restrict our issue today to four pages ... The local situation which has for the time being created disturbance of normal arrangements is well in hand, we are glad to say, and we hope that an ordinary issue of the *Straits Times* will be made tomorrow. Meantime we beg the indulgence of our readers. For the present, the matter of supreme interest is news from the seat of war and that news we present herewith.' Thus was the Sepoy Mutiny of the previous day announced to the residents of Singapore, with unruffled coolness, only to be immediately passed over as an event hardly worth noticing. Half the Indian troops of the 5th Light Infantry and 100 men of the Malay State Guides had mutinied and were wandering about the colony committing mayhem and murder.

But the event was noticed and caused wholesale panic among civilians and military of the city alike, in an anticipation of what would happen in the next war. In the language of the time, it was a 'total funk' or more militarily 'an absolute shambles' with the most extraordinary unpreparedness on all sides. Western ladies abandoned their houses and fled to the ships in the harbour, leaving their servants to fend for themselves. Since the mutiny broke out on a holiday, most of the men were on the golf course or at the club and expected to survive on sheer British pluck and hazy memories of the OTC. The colony was shockingly underdefended and complacent. The main difference was that this time the Japanese, in the form of trim and efficient marines, were within reach as allies and ready to prevent the tottering empire from falling. It marked a major change in their public image. Hitherto, Japanese in Singapore had been pimps and prostitutes. To the huge embarrassment of the British authorities, French and Russian marines also played a part in the suppression of the mutiny that was swiftly put down after all the initial dithering.

The first instinct, naturally, was to hush everything up. There was a swift court martial at which two sepoys were condemned to death and executed. Then there was a change of the official mind and it was decided that publicity was needed to serve as an example that might reassure the British residents and act as a warning to those wider currents of disaffection felt to be circulating among Muslim subjects especially. The men were tried in batches and 47 executions conducted by firing squad and nearly two hundred others receiving sentences of some kind. A single Muslim merchant, Kassim Al Mansoor, was convicted of treason through incitement and hanged. The court regretted that many of the outraged witnesses were ladies, unused to telling one Indian from another.

Then came a court of enquiry. We are now used to expensive and exhaustive inquiries that reveal that senior levels were clear of all incompetence and responsibility and that somehow any blame was a purely local matter. That following the Sepoy Mutiny followed this well-run course. The mutiny had been caused by recent lack of discipline and the activities of obscure, foreign agents who sought to foster discontent. The alleged special relationship between officers and men in the Indian Army had acquired an almost holy status. Then there had been trouble-makers among the troops who spread rumours that they were to be posted – not as had been claimed to Hong Kong – but to Europe where they would fight Turkish fellow-Muslims.

But it was odd that one of the first acts of the mutineers had been to liberate the German prisoners of war held in the Tanglin barracks. The court downplayed their part in the mutiny, despite the evidence of collusion between them and the regiment that had provided their guards, but it was felt that this, at least, was the origin of the fiery speeches of German ascendancy with which one of the ringleaders harangued his men before the mutiny. Any small blame available was rather to be attached to the officers of the cruiser *Emden* who had conveniently absconded from the prison and were unavailable for interrogation as they made the long trip back to Germany. In the responses of both the Governor and the Commanding Officer of the Singapore forces to the report of the enquiry, it became clear that it had long been feared that the Indian troops had been 'tampered with' by the German prisoners and it had been decided that henceforth only white troops should guard them, an instruction that was never followed through. It was also the case that the Indian guards were convinced that the Germans had themselves converted to Islam, a view in which they had been encouraged by openly kneeling in prayer at sunset and the pretended reading of the Koran. Some of the men from the *Emden* would subsequently write their own memoirs, notably Julius Lauterbach – a larger than life character – who was one of the escapees. In the various books in which he was later involved, he is evasive, admitting to knowing of the mutinous feelings of their guards but having done nothing to encourage them, then later claiming a much more active part in the events, indeed making the whole plan his own. Despite the government's denials, in Singapore itself, the feeling that he and his men lay behind the extraordinary events of 1915 never quite dissipated and generated ever-new rumours. The Governor felt compelled to address and dismiss them in his annual review of the year 1915. And he was especially firm in discrediting the allegations that some of the sepoys were found to be in possession of gold sovereigns that could only have been bribes from the affluent German civilians of the camp. The response of the home government did nothing to lay speculation to rest. It sequestered the official documents relating to the affair and made them publicly inaccessible for years to come.

We will never know exactly what lay behind the confused events of the 1915 Singapore Sepoy mutiny. Was it due to the deeper undercurrents of the Ghadr party's worldwide conspiracy to free India from British rule? Or was it the purely local matter of a regimental clash of personalities in a remote barracks far from home? Or was it the result of a the playful, bragging of a German naval officer, with what many held to be an excessive and diseased sense of humour, who joked outrageously to his batman that Germany had converted to Islam? Whatever the source, it caused ferment in Singapore and began that undermining of the myths of empire that would finally collapse with fortress Singapore in the next conflagration.

What impresses in the present account is the strength of that self-confidence in a world that has completely disappeared. All empires depend on bluff and self-delusion and a certain blinkeredess of viewpoint that makes possible acts of courage that would be impossible to a wider vision. The court of inquiry remarked that 'The time-honoured maxim of *l'audace toujours l'audace* when dealing with Orientals was apparently lost sight of' as if this were an unquestionable truth. Despite all the complexities of the case, it seems that it was all really a matter of British pluck. Certainly, the writer of this eye-witness account would have agreed with that.

Nigel Barley, author
Rogue Raider: the tale of Captain Lauterbach, the Singapore Mutiny and the audacious Battle of Penang

Foreword

Celia Ferguson

There is a rood screen in St Andrew's Cathedral, Singapore, dedicated to my grandfather, Major Edwin Arthur Brown, OBE, VD, JP, and his wife, Mary, who died in internment in Sumatra in January 1945. It was hard to find as the commemoration brass plaque was often hidden under a pile of hymn books. It was sad to think that someone who was the backbone of Singapore for 40 years was reduced to a brass plaque that couldn't easily be seen. I was therefore particularly delighted that his book *Indiscreet Memories* was republished by Monsoon Books, and his eight grandchildren have since replaced the brass plaque with a larger one which is better sited in honour of the revived interest in his great contribution to the betterment of life in Singapore.

But *Indiscreet Memories* has brought about the publication of this very interesting book, his first hand account of the Singapore Mutiny in February 1915. I well remember the excitement when it first came into my life as a young girl in Northern Ireland in the 1950s. My grandfather, known throughout Singapore as EAB, had arrived there in January 1901, aged 23, to work for a German firm called Brinkmanns, which was a subsidiary of Hiltermann Brothers of Manchester. He was one of only two Englishmen at the outset, although more were to come until eventually they outnumbered the German employees. In the early days as a bachelor, EAB rented a room in the Hotel de la Paix in Coleman Street, and later in Zetland House in Armenian Street. He quickly got to be well known and invited out to the homes of other expats and became a popular and useful addition to many aspects of life in Singapore. He soon joined the Singapore Volunteers and eventually became a Major and was awarded the Volunteer Decoration medal. While he was a Captain, he was caught up in the Singapore Mutiny and took an active part in quelling it. He wrote this long account of that eventful episode, in his own hand in great detail, and dedicated it to my mother, born in Singapore in October 1911 and aged 3 at the time of the Mutiny. My grandmother enlivened his account by interspersing it with her own concurrent experiences, while coping with a small child – my mother – and her dread of anything happening to her beloved Eddie comes through very clearly. By reading the story from both the military and the civilian standpoints, one gets a very full picture of this historic event in Singapore's history which, in EAB's words, could so easily have gone the other way with disastrous and far wider reaching consequences.

This stirring account, along with all the family belongings, was presumed lost forever with the Japanese invasion of Singapore. Miraculously, several years after the Japanese Occupation and EAB's release from the civilian prison in Changi and return from Singapore to the UK, the handwritten manuscript turned up at a second-hand shop in Singapore and was spotted by someone who knew him and sent it to him. He and my mother were so delighted at the time and there was great interest in the book.* As his eldest grandchild, I have the original and the Imperial War Museum in London has a copy.

When EAB arrived in Singapore, he was a clever and enterprising young man of adventurous nature who wanted to see the world and seek his fortune. He was brought up near Manchester and went to the very prestigious Hulme Grammar School. He was one of a family of two brothers and three sisters who were all very talented musically and artistically, and he had the most marvellous singing voice which, if he had decided to sing as a profession, would undoubtedly have brought him fame and fortune. But he chose to go into business and he chose Singapore as his destination, while his brother went to Canada to live the life of a pioneer settler, building himself a log cabin to live in.

EAB did better than his brother, as in 1910, having done well in business, he got engaged to his old friend Mary Hobbins, and built a beautiful house in Rochalie Drive for his bride, calling it Burnsall after the village where they spent their honeymoon. The Brown and Hobbins families were very close friends and all gifted in various fields of the Arts. EAB, Mary and their siblings, as teenagers, together edited and produced a wonderfully artistic and clever magazine which they called "The Ivy Leaf" or "I Cling to Thee!"

It was also not long after EAB's arrival before he hit the amateur dramatic scene, having left Manchester with a certain amount of fame after a string of hits on the stage there in a semi-professional capacity over two years before leaving for Singapore. Of course he was a hit in Singapore too and it used to be said that EAB put the Sing in Singapore! He was a man who knew his own mind and was pretty autocratic! This was often experienced by the choir members while he was the honorary Choirmaster in St Andrew's Cathedral for 40 years, and once they turned the tables on him by paraphrasing the words of an old hymn and singing "Not Thy will but mine be done O Lord"! He founded and ran the Singapore Musical Society and produced and took leading roles in several Gilbert and Sullivan Operas and in 1923 he founded the Children's Orchestra. Both he and

Mary were crack shots and had a huge array of trophies and silver cups for rifle shooting, and were many times the Malayan champions. He was the Chief Commissioner for Scouts and a great encourager of scouting.

For some 13 years EAB served the community as a Municipal Commissioner, with responsibilities for many of the Singapore services such as roads, drainage, the fire brigade etc. He was particularly interested in assisting the Malays, Chinese and Indians and especially the children. He had many close friends in these communities and spoke fluent Malay and Mandarin. He campaigned for and achieved the creation of the Municipal Baths and a public park – the People's Park (now Katong Park) – for the benefit of the poor people, and installed bandstands so that music could be enjoyed by them. He organised a huge gathering of children for the visit of the Prince of Wales – later King Edward VIII – to Singapore. As the Prince of Wales was leaving, all the children sang "God Bless the Prince of Wales" and he stopped to listen. EAB was always active, and even after the Japanese had entered the mainland of Malaya, he was given the job of organising the reception in Singapore of refugees fleeing from the advancing Japanese forces.

All this was of course voluntary work. As far as business was concerned, EAB left Brinkmanns in 1918 and set up an Exchange Broking business, EA Brown & Co., with a

Scotsman, Iain McLeod (known as Mac) and an Indian partner. They were very successful and invested heavily – as many did – in the rapidly growing rubber industry.

He and Mary had 3 children – the eldest was Barbara, my mother, born in 1911; then Shelagh, born in 1916 and finally Alec in 1919. They were all sent home to be brought up by grandmothers and aunts when Alec was a baby and my mother had to go to school. It must have been heartbreaking for my grandparents, but it was not considered a healthy place to nurture children in those days, and the mothers had to choose between their husband and their children. The journey home took a month, so Mary only saw her children every 3 years or so. EAB's investments in the rubber industry lost him a fortune in the financial slump of the early 1930s, just when he was planning to move back to England and buy a lovely family house in their beloved Southwold in Suffolk, so that the family could be reunited. Instead, he and Mary stayed in Singapore and one of the jobs EAB then undertook was to be the Singapore Film Censor.

After Burnsall, Rochalie Road, they lived in the 1920s in a house called The Grange in Meyer Road, and in the 1930s moved to Grove Court, 48 Goodman Road, Katong, with a large lake with crocodiles. Barbara and Shelagh came to join them there in 1936 and Shelagh worked in the Naval Office while Barbara, my mother, worked for the Police

Special Branch. In April 1939, my parents were married in St Andrew's Cathedral, Singapore. My father, then Lt Cdr Claud Herdman, was stationed in the Naval Offiice in Singapore, and the wedding was a great social occasion for Singapore. I have a colour film of the occasion, taken by Robert (Bobby) Waddle who was the Cathedral Organist at the time. When the Japanese invaded, he put all his films down the biggest pipe of the Cathedral organ and, after surviving nearly 4 years internment in Changi, he was able to retrieve them intact in late 1945.

My parents came home to the UK before the war, but unfortunately my grandparents and Shelagh were stuck in Singapore as it was so risky to travel after war broke out. Alec was captured at Dunkirk and interned in Germany for the rest of the war in Europe. When the Japanese invaded, Mary and Shelagh were evacuated on the *Vyner Brooke*, but it was bombed and sunk and they both survived and were interned in Sumatra. EAB in the meantime was interned in Changi where he went from 16 ½ stone down to 8 ¼ stone, in spite of being cared for by his old house staff who loyally did the best they could in bringing gifts of food, etc. When he was released it was to learn that Shelagh had also survived her ordeal, but his beloved Mary had died in January 1945. He never really talked about her again, although he lived until 1955. He had lost everything of course, and spent the rest of his life spending 6 months of every year with us in Northern Ireland and 6 months with his sisters in Kent. (Shelagh had married the Rev. Arthur Lea and was living in Canada and Alec, too, had married Machili Kirkman and was in the Colonial Police in Nigeria.)

EAB continued to be involved with music, setting up a very successful choir in Strabane, Co Tyrone, which survived for decades after his death. He was also a clever carpenter and spent hours at his workbench in our garage, wearing fingerless gloves, making me a lovely wooden dolls house and furniture; a fort and a garage for my brothers and all sorts of other wonderful toys, money boxes, lamps and carved hanging bookshelves for all his children and grandchildren. I can still picture him making a semi-circular hearth rug by hand, cutting the wool meticulously and knotting it with a special hook. Sadly his sight went and he became rather dispirited as a result, eventually dying in 1955 of heart trouble in a nursing home in Stroud, Gloucestershire, where Alec and family had settled shortly before. I am so thankful now that I had the privilege and pleasure of having my loving and much loved Grandpa live with us for half the year until I was 12 years old.

Regrettably, I never knew my grandmother because of her internment and death in Sumatra. With other civilians whose graves the British declined to move (only those with military connections were moved), she is buried beneath a petrol station and housing development on Muntok Island. Her spirit lives on in the amazing music of the prison camp "Vocal Orchestra" immortalised in the film *Paradise Road* and in which she and Aunt Shelagh sang, and also the book *Women Beyond the Wire* by Lavinia Warner and John Sandilands tells the story of their long ordeal and her eventual death. She knew that I had been born in June 1943, thanks to the only correspondence that reached them in 3 years, and that was a postcard from an old friend with the news of my safe arrival. She made me a beautiful doll with scraps she earned by undertaking tasks for her Dutch fellow prisoners – and it is probably my most treasured possession.

Mrs Celia Ferguson MBE (née Herdman),
Sion Mills, Co. Tyrone, N. Ireland

*I have letters to my mother from RWE Harper in 1970, and Harry Miller in 1974, who collaborated in writing their account of the Singapore Mutiny. I also have a letter from FT Wynyard-Wright in 1974 saying the official account quoted in a letter to *The Times* by Harry Miller did not agree with his experience.

Contents

Glossary

Amok	Malay expression for running wild or on the rampage.
Blakan Mati	former name of Sentosa Island.
Jaga	slang for guard (from the Malay for guard, 'penjaga').
Kebun	Slang for gardener (from the Malay for gardener, 'tukang kebun').
Mem	Colonial-era form of address for the lady of the house, Mistress.
Pulo Brani	former spelling of an island between Singapore and Sentosa islands
Syce	a person who takes care of horses; a groom.
Tuan	Malay for sir, master.

A Note on Names

Edwin A. Brown appears in the diary as Edwin, Eddie, Edd, Ed and EAB. Mary Brown appears in the diary as Mary and Molly. Barbara Brown appears in the diary as Barbara and Baba.

A Note on Spelling

Spelling and punctuation have been left in the original.

Military Abbreviations

5th LI	5th Light Infantry
COL	Colonel
DAAG	Deputy Assistant Adjutant General
GSO	General Staff Officer
GSO1	General Staff Officer (Grade 1)
GSO2	General Staff Officer (Grade 2)
IGP	Inspector General of Police
Lt	Lieutenant
Lt Col	Lieutenant-Colonel
MSG	Malay States Guides
MSVR	Malay States Volunteer Rifles
OC	Officer Commanding. Brigadier-General Ridout was GOC Troops, Singapore (General Officer Commanding the Troops, Singapore) in 1915.
QMG	Quartermaster General
RAMC	Royal Army Medical Corps
RE	Royal Engineers
RGA	Royal Garrison Artillery

List of Persons Killed by Mutineers

Military personnel killed by mutineers

5TH LIGHT INFANTRY
Captain P. Boyce, double company comander
Lieutenant H. S. Elliot, company comander

ROYAL GARRISON ARTILLERY
Major F. V. Izard
Captain R. H. Galwey
Corporal J. R. V. Beagley

ROYAL ARMY SERVICE CORPS
Sergeant F. H. Sexton

JOHORE MILITARY FORCES
Captain H. Cullimore
Captain Abdul Jabar
Private Yaacob bin Salleh

MALAY STATES GUIDES (ARTILLERY UNIT)
Battery Commander, Captain M. F. A. Maclean, RA

SINGAPORE VOLUNTEER GUIDES
Lieutenant A. F. Legge (medical officer)
Sergeant G. O. Lawson
Sergeant G. Wald
Lance-Corporal J. C. Harper
Private B. C. Cameron
Private A Drysdale
Private A. J. G. Holt

MALAY STATES VOLUNTEER RIFLES (DETACHMENT)
Commandant of the German prisoner-of-war camp,
    Captain P. N. Gerrard
Second-Lieutenant J. H. Love-Montgomerie
Private W. H. Leigh

Prison service personnel killed by mutineers

Warder J. Clarke (fatally wounded)

Civilians killed by mutineers

Mr E. O. Butterworth

Mr H. B. Collins

Mr H. O'Shaughnessey Collins

Mr J. B. Dunn

Mr C. V. Dyson

Mr N. F. Edwards

Mr A. R. Evans

Mr F. Geddes (died of wounds)

Mr Hassan Kechil bin Hassan

Mrs Lim Eng Wee

Mr D. McGilvray

Mr W. J. Marshall

Mr Omar bin Ahmad Kaptin

Mr E. F. Senftleben (a German prisoner of war, killed by mutineers during their attack on the camp)

Mr C. Smith

Mrs Sim Soh

Dr E. D. Whittle

Mr and Mrs G. B. Woolcombe

Unidentified Chinese male

List of Maps

Letter from Edwin A. Brown

to his daughter, Barbara, 1924

5.10.1924

My dear Barbara,

I am finishing the transcribing of the notes made by Mummy and myself many years after the exciting incidents occurred to the three of us. I am sitting at a little table in the deckhouse of a cargo ship in the Indian Ocean, homeward bound, and the events contained in this book seem now a very long way off. But at the time, dear, it was very real trouble, and on looking back upon it all now it seems that only a very small thing saved us from a terrible disaster on that 15th day of February 1915. That was the action of Admiral Jerram, who was in Singapore at the time, and who so promptly turned out the sailors off the little Gunboat in harbour, and sent them down to Pasir Panjang towards

Alexandra, with orders to shoot at sight anything they saw with a rifle.

They killed several mutineers that afternoon, who were straggling about the roads, and we found out afterwards that among them was the Ringleader of the mutiny, a very able native officer of the Regiment. If that man had lived, the result of our attack on Alexandra the next morning might have had a very different ending, for if that funny little force of Col Brownlow's had been beaten back then, God only knows what would have happened to Singapore.

Later on, Russian, French, and Japanese Cruisers were rushed to the spot and landed their men, and the 5th Shropshire Light Infantry were hurried from Rangoon, so we were safe.

But those first few days were days of excitement and risk, and Mummy and I feel that, as you grow older, it will interest you to read the full account of a most exciting time in your life, although you were so young then that you probably have but a vague recollection, if any, of the events chronicled here.

So we have written this account for you, and now present it to you with our love, in the hope that you will find interest in reading it.

Though there were lots of other happenings worth writing about during the 'clearing up' of the mutiny, they are better kept for 'round the fire' stories, as they occurred when the crisis was over.[1]

So we leave the tale as it stands, and perhaps in days to come you will pick up this book, and read once again with interest of the time when you were a refugee on a ship and went through the troublous days of what will always be known as 'The Singapore Mutiny'.

Your ever loving
Daddy

[1] Edwin A. Brown did pen the round-the-fire clearing-up stories and they appear in this book in the chapter 'Cleaning Up'.

Revolt

Edwin A. Brown

Chinese New Year 1915 will long be remembered in the Straits Settlements. As usual at that time of the year general holidays had been proclaimed, and the godowns were for the most part shut. My company of Volunteers, the Chinese, had been given thirty hours leave from duty – they were doing guards at various points on the island – and on the Thursday morning, the 15th, I remobilized ninety-two men, and accompanied them to Johnson's Pier, from which point they left by launch for the islands of Pulo Brani and Blakan Mati, for guard duty.

After getting this business over, and seeing the men safely off, Mary and Miss Stiles, who had been down to see the Company fall in, and myself, left for home again, had a tiffin, and went to our rooms for a lie-off, having arranged to go for a good walk when the heat of the day was over. To notice it, I cannot say which, we had our tea, and at 5pm got into the trap, which was to take us to a point from which we were going to walk home. I think that at this point it will be necessary to give a diagram of the roads round about the Barracks, so that the situation can be better understood:

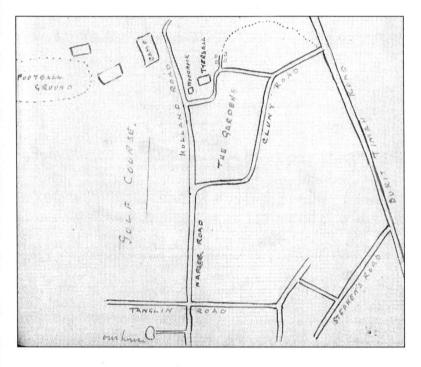

Above Original sketch by Edwin A. Brown.
Opposite Edwin A. Brown's map with transcribed names.

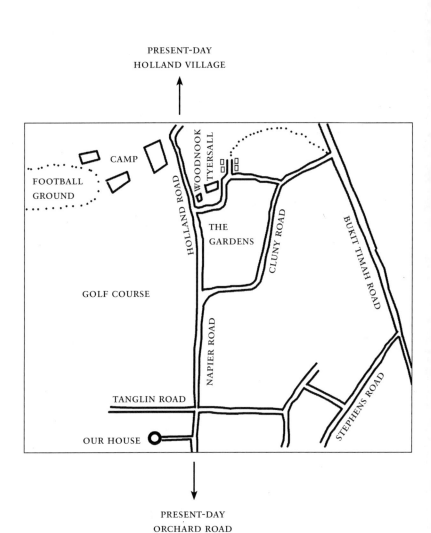

PRESENT-DAY
HOLLAND VILLAGE

CAMP

FOOTBALL
GROUND

WOODNOOK

TYERSALL

HOLLAND ROAD

THE
GARDENS

CLUNY ROAD

BUKIT TIMAH ROAD

GOLF COURSE

NAPIER ROAD

TANGLIN ROAD

STEPHENS ROAD

OUR HOUSE

PRESENT-DAY
ORCHARD ROAD

We drove along Tanglin Road, into Stephens Road, and along Bukit Timah Road to the junction of Cluny Road and Bukit Timah Road, and there we dismissed the trap, sending the syce straight back to the yard, because our own stables required new boards, and a horse could not at the moment be put into them. (This is a little matter you'll think, but nevertheless it became an important one later.)

Then we started for our walk. Getting off the main road, we followed a country footpath where the dotted line is seen in the plan until we came again into a small residential district. We thought it a curious fact that no-one was playing tennis, and that the few houses there were seemed to be shut up, but did not bother much about it, and went on down the road, leaving Tyersall, the Singapore residence of the Sultan of Johore, on our right, until we came to Woodnook, a smaller house standing in the same grounds, and one generally used by the Sultan.

There were more natives about here, and they seemed to be excited about something, but we knew the Sultan of Johore was expected in Singapore with his troops that day, and we thought that he was probably staying there. Everything, you see, had an easy explanation that afternoon, and yet, had we known it, we would probably have found there Corporal

Todd, with the two Europeans and about forty Malay troops, whom by his presence of mind he had saved from the massacre.

Getting down to the corner of Holland Road, I suggested to Mary and Miss Stiles that we should walk along to the corner by the German Encampment, as I had never seen the Camp, so on we went. As we drew near, Mary, who had seen it before, remarked that it was curious that no guards were to be seen on the Sentinel towers. It was only then that I began to get an uneasy feeling that all was not as it should be, and I suggested turning back again.

What would have happened if we had gone on I don't know. We turned back, and my uneasiness increased when we noticed that there was not a soul to be seen on the Garrison Golf Course. I said nothing about it to the others however, but walked on, and it was only when we got to the cross roads at Tanglin, and met a motor lorry disgorging a mixture of RE [Royal Engineers], RGA [Royal Garrison Artillery] and Volunteers, in all stages of undress, that we got our first real intimation that something serious was the matter.

I asked one of the men the trouble, but he wouldn't tell me, even if he knew – which I doubt – so we rushed home, and there I found that the telephone had been ringing for me for an hour.

Mary got through to the Drill Hall, while I jumped into a pair of shorts, putties and a shirt; I ate a sandwich and had a drink, and by that time Wreford, our friend, whom we had rung up, had come round with his car to get me down to the Drill Hall. Even then, you must understand, nothing had been said about any danger, and I was almost inclined to think the whole thing was a practice alarm, or else at the worst a few German prisoners had escaped.

When we were ready to go I told Molly not to worry, I'd be back soon, if not to dinner, soon after, and off I went with Wreford. On approaching town, the car was held up by a police officer who directed Wreford to drive to the P&O Wharf, as soon as he had dropped me, as all cars were requisitioned. That was worrying news, and I then began to think of Molly, and asked Wreford to go for her if there was any danger. He promised to do so, but we couldn't think of what danger there could be. You can imagine my horror when I got to the Drill Hall and found that the 5th LI [Light Infantry] had broken out in open mutiny and had been in Tanglin that afternoon, and were even then supposed to be marching on Singapore!!

In spite of the fact that the telephone had been in constant use, I got through to Mary and told her to come down to the Chinese Girls' School or one of the Hotels at once, it was urgent that she should do so. I daren't tell her what had happened even then. Her experiences in getting down that night we will leave for a later chapter.

History of the Outbreak

Edwin A. Brown

The history of the outbreak, as far as one is able to piece things together from the evidence at the trials etc. is as follows.

The 5th Light Infantry had been in Singapore since the departure of the 3rd Brahmins. It was not considered a particularly high class regiment, but it was an old established one, and part of it, at all events, could point to some faithful work during the Indian Mutiny. It was a "one class" regiment, that is to say the men composing it were all of one religion and caste, contrary to the general rule in most regiments where there are generally more than two classes of men.

An Indian Regiment is divided into Right and Left Wings, each Wing consisting of two Double Companies of about 200 men each, commanded by a Captain, who is mounted. The fighting strength of such a regiment is therefore about 800 men, but besides this there are numerous camp followers, such as coolies, dobies, syces, and odds and ends, even including tailors, and the total strength of the regiment as it moves from station to station is round about 1000. These camp followers are generally of the same religion, but of a lower caste than the fighting men. A rough and ready, but useful, rule for the European to remember as regards Indian caste is, that the higher the caste, the less menial work it is permitted to do, so the necessity of camp followers, such as those mentioned, among a lot of men who consider themselves "Somebody" can be recognized immediately.

So much for the composition of the regiment that mutinied, and now to explain briefly the dispositions of the military forces throughout the Island.

The OC Troops Singapore [Officer Commanding the Troops in Singapore] was Col Ridout, an Engineer officer, with experience in the South African War. (He was promoted to Brigadier-General on the day of the mutiny, his promotion arriving from the War Office at midnight.) Under him were two Lieutenant Colonels, one of the RAMC [Royal Army Medical Corps] named Ferguson, and Lt Col Brownlow of the RGA, an old Indian Frontier fighter who had spent much of his life with a mountain battery, taking part in those "little wars" which one doesn't hear much about but which have done so much to keep the Indian Empire together. The Regulars in the place consisted of some RAMC men, about 40 RE, and 200 RGA, 100 of which were the Sikh

Co of the Hongkong and Singapore Battalion RGA. (The White Regiment had been moved some time ago and was by this time well in the forefront of the fight in France.) Then there were a few negligible details of Army Pay Dept, Staff Sergeants etc, and a small detachment under a Lieutenant of the Army Service Corps.

As regards the Volunteers, the SVC (Singapore Volunteer Corps) consisted at this time of the following:

SVA [Singapore Volunteer Artillery]
   – about 60 officers and men

SRE(v) [Singapore Royal Engineers (Volunteers)]
   – about 40 officers and men

SVI [Singapore Volunteer Infantry]
   Chinese – about 120 officers and men
   Malay – about 120 officers and men

Besides these, there was the newly formed Company of the Volunteer Rifles, a body of Europeans who at this time had never fired a rifle, and who had had practically no instruction in it, but knew something about Drill, and to finish up with there was the Veteran Company, the "Old 'uns", who had done a few drills without arms, but who, as a body, knew nothing whatever about the rifle. These two Companies, nominally 100 strong each, could muster about 150 men between them.

The last remaining unit to be mentioned, but not by any means the least, was a company of the MSVR [Malay States Volunteer Rifles], who were down in Singapore doing a month's training under their Captain, Sidney Smith. This company could be considered as a fairly useful body of men, most of them in excellent bodily condition (being planters etc), and trained above the average for volunteers of this description.

As regards the dispositions of the troops at the time of the outbreak, they were roughly as follows.

The RGA were all on Blakan Mati, the fortified island lying opposite the docks. The RE, including the Volunteers of the same arm, were on Pulo Brani, an adjacent island, the Volunteers being there especially for Searchlight duty. On these islands too was practically the whole of the Chinese Co SVI, doing duty as guards at the various ports, and lastly some details of the RAMC and AOB were also stationed there.

The 5th Light Infantry were in their Barracks, the Native Infantry Barracks at Alexandra Road, some four and a half to five miles out of town, and the smaller encampment on the Rifle Range adjoining Alexandra Barracks was occupied by the Company of the MSVR who were in Singapore for training. In Alexandra Barracks there was also the Mule Battery of the Malay States Guides, which regiment had been the cause of some uneasiness for some little time, and which had therefore been split up into detachments. (It is only fair to add that a large proportion of the Battery remained loyal during the mutiny.)

The Volunteers headquarters were at the Drill Hall in the town, and from there the various mobilized detachments were sent out to the posts which, at the outbreak of war, were given over to the Volunteers to guard. One of these posts was at the Prisoners of War Camp in Tanglin, and 2nd Lieut Montgomerie with 15 men had gone upon the Saturday for their spell of duty.

Owing to the imminent departure of the 5th LI for Hongkong, and the consequent shortage of troops in the Settlement, the Government had accepted the offer of the Sultan of Johore to provide assistance, and that Saturday the Sultan had arrived with about 300 men from his State. About 50 of them were sent on arrival to Tanglin as part of the prison guard but when they got there it was found that they required special ammunition which, as far as I can gather, they had not asked for until it was too late, and before supplies arrived at Tanglin the mutiny had broken out.

The last remaining detachment to refer to is a detail of the 36th Sikhs, who were passing through on their way to their regiment in Hongkong, when it was decided to send the regiment to France, and the detail was therefore stopped in Singapore until the regiment went through. These men were in a Barrack Room at Tanglin, of course without any ammunition.

And now to recount, as well as I can from accounts I have been told, the story of the outbreak. At about 2.30 pm on the Monday afternoon, when those officers who were in camp at Alexandra were having a "lie-off " after tiffin – it was a public holiday, they heard a rifle shot from the direction of the lines, and then another; and immediately afterwards the alarm bell was heard furiously ringing the "Assembly". Wondering what on earth could have happened, they rushed out in the direction of their various companies. Capt Hall's own account to me shows that when he reached his company's lines, he found about 150 men gathering together in a great state of excitement, with rifles in their hands but no ammunition (it must be understood that all ammunition had been called in preparatory to embarking on the morrow) and their first story to Hall was that one or two men were running "amok". This news was soon superseded by the news that the Quarter guard had been attacked, the magazine broken open, and that about half the regiment were supplying themselves with ammunition. Hall ordered his men to fall in, but almost immediately fire was opened upon them, and there was nothing for Hall to do but to order his men to disperse and get into the jungle nearby, and lie "doggo" for the present.

At this juncture Major Cotton and Capt Elliott appeared on the scene running hard, followed by scattered rifle fire, and Hall joined them. Cotton explained that he was off to try and warn the MSVR, and that one at all events of the three of them must get through and bring up the Volunteers – by this time it must have been 3 o'clock. Spreading out to about twenty paces interval and keeping low, away they went therefore, in little rushes, skirting the drill ground, and getting among some trees. It must have been just about here that poor Elliott was hit, for he called out to Hall "They've got me, Hall, but it's nothing much". He went on a bit after this, but then they never saw him again alive, and the conjecture is that he must have found that his wound would not allow him to keep up, and he had crept away to hide. That he was discovered by the devils however was proved by the awful wounds on his body when it was found, some days afterwards.

Cotton and Hall kept on, and after a bit the rifle fire slackened and died away in their direction, and they were able to go straight to the Barracks of the MSVR across the

Rifle Range.

Here they found Capt Smith and about seventy men of the MSVR – the rest were in town on leave. Within five minutes the men were collected, ammunition served out, and away the party went with the intention of getting to the Colonel's Bungalow, where, as far as they knew, the Colonel had remained. Crossing the Rifle Range, they reached the Officers' Mess undisturbed, and with a final rush attained the Colonel's house.

Here, curiously enough, they found everything undisturbed, for the mutineers, instead of rushing the house, as they might have done, and being in possession of it before the MSVR arrived, had contented themselves with pouring fire into the houses of the other officers, which were extended along the top of the ridge from the Colonel's Bungalow.

An officer's wife in one of these bungalows had a terrifying experience. When the firing began, her husband, Major Cotton, went off to the lines, and she did not think that anything serious had happened. After a bit however she heard shots hit the house, and so she collected her servants, and with them crept underneath the house, a bungalow. There she remained for a long time, with the mutineers firing shots into and through the house, with the evident intention of killing her. It was not until dusk that a rescue party could get out from the Colonel's Bungalow and bring her in.

No definite attack seems to have been made on the Colonel's Bungalow after the MSVR got there, but the mutineers besieged the place all night and kept up a desultory sniping at all the windows. There seem to have been a good many mutineers detailed for this work, but the actual number will never be ascertained.

While all this was being brought about, a strong party of the mutineers had left in the direction of Tanglin Barracks, with the evident intention of attacking the prison guard and releasing the German Prisoners. This move must have been made the moment the mutiny broke out, and as a matter of fact was the only organized move that the mutineers made. It is evident, therefore, that it had been arranged beforehand, and this point is one of the principal ones in the argument of those who favour the theory that the Germans were at the bottom of the trouble.

This party then left Alexandra for Tanglin about 2.30 to 3pm. They had some distance to go, across fairly rough country, but they made a bee-line for the place, and arrived at the back of the Hospital overlooking the Barracks recreation ground around 4pm.

Now it was the custom in the detention camp to take the Germans out of Barracks about this time each day for exercise in the Recreation Ground, which had been surrounded with corrugated iron for safety. On this Monday afternoon, therefore, the prisoners had been taken down as usual, guarded by a few Volunteers, and put into the recreation ground and the door locked on them, when suddenly a shot was heard, and then another, and then a scattered volley, and shots rattled on the corrugated, some going right through.

Corp. Todd, of the SVR [Singapore Volunteer Rifles] and a member of the Cathedral Choir, who seems to be the only man left of the unfortunate Volunteer guard who can give a coherent and connected story of all the events at Tanglin, tells me that the mutineers started firing at the men on the detention camp guard posts, which are raised platforms at each corner of the camp. One of the Malay guards went down at once, and the other two, having no ammunition left, seem to have evacuated their posts. The Volunteer on the other however kept up a steady fire until he too, poor chap, went down, and then began the indiscriminate slaughter that will long be remembered in this place. Cullimore, the British Instructor of the Johore forces, rushing out of his house to rouse his men, or find out what was the matter, was riddled with wounds and fiendishly bayonetted afterwards. Capt Gerrard the Detention Camp Officer (acting) was caught in his office and literally messed up. Poor Montgomerie of the Volunteers, after bravely warning people on the telephone of the trouble, was murdered on the steps of the Guard room, as everybody that could be seen was shot at. Pte Robertson of the Volunteers had a marvellous escape, a bullet cutting across his throat, but not going deep enough to do much damage. Streaming with blood, he rushed off in the direction of the Golf course to warn the players, and the sight of him as he came up was sufficient to show those playing that it was an extremely dangerous spot to be in. Volunteers and others got the ladies away then rushed off to their Headquarters, warning residents as they went.

In the meantime, Corp.Todd, who was near the gate of the Recreation Ground, had rushed inside, where the Germans were running about like rabbits, and warned them to lie down. The mutineers had evidently seen him go in, for shots again began to come through the corrugated iron, and Todd thought he had best get out again. So opening the gate he made a rush, and succeeded in gaining the cover of some buildings where he picked up two Volunteers. They kept up a fire on the mutineers for some time, but then saw them creeping round to their right, and fearful of being cut off, and not seeing what good three men could do under the circumstances, he decided to retire. He seems to have done this with discretion, and the mutineers, here, as elsewhere, hesitated to attack even three men, who were at bay. In their retreat they came across the dead bodies of some more of the guard, and saw one of their comrades standing in the middle of the road, wildly waving his arms. Todd called to him to take cover but to no purpose, and the next moment he too fell, riddled with bullets. They think the poor fellow had gone mad. Soon after this the three Volunteers were joined by about forty Malay troops (Johore) without ammunition and in a terrible state of funk. They also picked up a wounded Malay. Todd seems to have handled the force well, as all this time they were under fire, and the mutineers were endeavouring to outflank them. The party eventually got across the road and up the hill on the other side into "Woodnook", from where they got into communication by telephone with the Drill Hall, and Todd and his two Volunteers were ordered to make their way back as quickly as possible to town. They eventually got in, after a roundabout tramp.

In the meantime, in the melee, one German prisoner had been shot and was in a dying condition, and one was seriously wounded, probably by bullets intended for Todd.

As soon as Todd's covering fire on the gate ceased, owing to the retreat of his party, the mutineers seem to have gone up to it, opened it, and gone in and shaken hands with the Germans, handing them rifles and ammunition. They evidently believed – whether they had been led to do so or not is not known – that the few hundred Germans there would immediately join them. To the credit of the Germans let it be said here that they refused as a body. Some fifteen of them got away later, and eleven of these made good their escape from the island, the rest being recaptured, but the great mass of the prisoners, even although they were without food for a whole day, remained in their camp. It is possible that the fifteen who escaped, being for the most part *Emden* and *Markomannia* men, including the notorious Diehn, of Behn Mayer and Co, may have had a hand in the rising, but it is certain that the general crowd in the camp knew nothing about it.

And so ended the slaughter at Tanglin. About eleven Volunteers had gone to their last account, foully murdered, and some Regulars had also been done to death, and it is certain that, if Corp. Todd had not kept his head, not only he and his two men, but the Johore Volunteers as well, would have been added to the list.

While all this had been going on, mutineers had been wandering about the roads on the outskirts of the town, shooting all white people they met. Capt Izard and Major Galway were both playing golf at Sepoy lines when they heard of the mutiny. They rushed off, one on a bicycle and the other in a rickshaw, to get back to the islands to their men, and were met and murdered on the way. Woolcolme and his wife were held up in their motor car and shot at point blank range. Dr Whittle was also with his wife in a motor car when he was shot; (how she escaped is a marvel), and the same happened to Dr Wald. His wife and baby of a year old were with him, and a bullet is said to have grazed the baby's forehead, while his wife had a bullet through her blouse and one through her hair and was unharmed! The devils entered several houses and shot men lying in long chairs, in one house killing three men in this manner.

And so they went on, thinking no doubt that they had Singapore at their mercy, when all the time Retribution was creeping swiftly upon them.

Escape

Mary Brown

When Eddie left the house at 7 o'clock to meet Mr Wreford in his car, I walked some little way along Grange Road with him and then turned to come back again. There was a strange stillness everywhere; I noticed that the houses were all in darkness and that there was not a soul about the roads. A rickshaw coolie kept close to me as I walked back, and as I began to feel a wee bit creepy, I got into the rickshaw and came home. I did not realize that anything serious was the matter. When I got back to the house again, Miss Stiles said the Drill Hall had been ringing up again for Edd and she had told them that he had left. I blame them very much for not telling Edd to bring his women-folk down with him, or at least informing him that there was serious trouble. It must be remembered that the mutiny started at 3.30pm, and it was after seven o'clock by the time Edd left the house. The whole regiment of the 5th LI was at large, and I shudder to think what might have been our fate here in the house with the doors all wide open, and we absolutely unprotected, and all the houses round about closed up. Our house was the only one in Tanglin that had any lights burning.

Well, to return to the narrative of the events of the evening; on arriving at the house, Baba [Barbara] was going to bed, so I heard her say her prayers and popped her into bed, and then we had our baths. When I was partly dressed the telephone bell rang again, and it was Eddie ringing me up from the Drill Hall, and this is what he said. "Molly, there is trouble among the natives, and you must get yourself, Baba, and Amah down to Raffles Hotel. Get away at once; I don't know how you can manage, but ring up someone to lend you a car." I said "Couldn't we go to Mrs Fowler's, she will take us in?" (little thinking that Mrs Fowler's house was shut up) but Eddie said "No, you aren't safe there; get away at once dear, I can't stay any longer as they want to use the telephone, good bye." I said "Where are you going to?" and the answer came back "I don't know." I put the receiver down and gasped for a moment or two, and then Eddie's words "You aren't safe in the house" rang in my ears, so I knew that it was up to me to get us all into a safe place as soon as possible, and it was a time for action, and quick action too, and there was no help to come from Eddie.

So first of all I rang up Raffles Hotel and tried to engage a room for one night. Raffles replied that they were sorry, they were full up and couldn't let me have a room, or even part of one. I replied that I was the wife of Capt Brown of the SVI and I was alone in Tanglin with my small child, and I considered that I was one of those who ought to be looked after before the people who had their husbands with them to help them. (I had no time or patience to mince matters, you see.) Raffles' reply to this argument was that I had better get down to town at all events, and they'd do their best for me. The next thing was to find means of transport. I rang up Mr Wreford, and asked for a lift in his car. He replied that he was at the moment taking six people down in it, but if I could wait he could send it back for me. So I said we would wait, as it ought to be back in half an hour's time. I then told Amah to get together as many of Baba's things as possible, and the boy put some of my clothes together and Miss Stiles kindly collected some tins of milk, and some Bovril and biscuits for Baba, and the whole collection was jumbled into a suit-case.

In the meantime I had got myself dressed, and so had Miss Stiles. The half hour had more than gone by by this but no car had appeared, and I began to grow uneasy, fearing that it must have had a breakdown or an accident of some sort (which was the case, as a tyre had burst just when the car was most wanted, of course). So I rang up the Motor Garage intending to hire one, but was informed that every single one of their cars had been commandeered by Government. This was serious news indeed, and you can imagine our feelings, hearing it while we were still in a deserted neighbourhood outside the town. It must be remembered that even yet we had heard nothing of the reasons for the trouble, and all sorts of things filled our imaginations.

However we had to get busy, (as the Americans say), so Miss Stiles and I began, by telephone, a house to house search for a car. I held the receiver and did the telephoning, and she looked up the various numbers in the book. We must have stood at the telephone for more than half an hour, but every house we could get through to sent back the same reply – from the houseboy – that the 'mem' and 'tuan' had gone away and were not coming back. I began to be very uneasy indeed now, and did not know whatever to do next. I told the boy to lock up all the doors of the house except the front ones; I left the lights in there in case the car came. I was just ringing up another house as a last chance of getting a car, when Mr Wreford's car at last arrived, but with only the native syce in it.

It did not take a minute to wrap Baba up in Golf jerseys and a blanket, and pop her socks and shoes on. The bag was put in the car and Miss Stiles and Amah got in the back, and I, with Baba asleep in my arms, seated myself next the chauffeur. I had given 'James' my keys and just walked out of the house leaving the place as it stood, and I told James to take care of everything until we came back.

We now set off into the deserted roads on our journey to Singapore. It was one of the blackest of black nights, with no moon. The car simply flew along, and it took us less time than usual to get to Singapore, speed limits were done away with altogether. I cannot tell you how relieved I was to see the town lights, the roads outside had been so black, and we were of course very nervous as even then we did not know what was the matter.

We arrived at Raffles at 9.40pm. The Hotel was simply crowded with people, nearly all women and children, and it was here that we first heard the news that the 5th LI had mutinied. Most of the women and children were sitting in the dining-room getting some food (we by the way had had no dinner, as we had been far too busy telephoning to eat). We found out where our room was first of all – it was on the ground floor – and I carried Baba to it. She was so heavy, it is no joke carrying 3 stone about in this climate, and the weight of blankets and clothes made things worse. The room was a long way off, but we reached it at last, absolutely dripping with perspiration; it was just as if I had been dipped – clothes and all – into a pail of water, my hair and everything about me was soaking.

Getting Baba into bed woke her up a little, but I explained to her that she was going to have a treat and sleep in Mummy's bed, and she soon snuggled down again and went off into a sound sleep very quickly. Miss Stiles and I then took it in turns to go and find out any news we could. What we heard was that several people we knew had been shot, and that there were eight hundred mutineers marching on the town. I knew that if this was so Edd would have gone out with the others to meet them. The suspense was simply terrible for one knew that at the most there could not be more than two hundred men with any military training at all to go and meet them, and of these, more than half of them were nothing more than Volunteer recruits. There only seemed to be one thing possible, humanly speaking, and that was that our men would be wiped out, and then we did not like to think what our fate would be. We did not seem to think of ourselves at all, but only of our men, and we could do nothing but wait and pray that they might be kept safe. Miss Stiles and I sat down in the little verandah of our room and thought we were settled for the night. Amah I sent to bed, and she was sleeping in one bed in the room and Baba in the other, with us just outside the door. I locked all the doors at the back of the room for safety's sake.

After a short time one of the men from the office came and found me, and asked if I had had all I wanted. He had just come in from a motor ride to the other side of the Island (opposite to the mutiny end), having gone to fetch

Mr Cunliffe in, who was staying the weekend out there. He was in the Hotel for a few minutes, getting his wife settled, preparatory to going out and offering his services as an armed civilian. I thanked him for his kindness, and he sent us a plate of sandwiches, and some lemonade and ginger ale, to which he had added a dash of brandy, which was very sensible of him, as we must have looked, and certainly felt, wrecks.

We had only eaten a sandwich or two when we heard an awful screaming going on in the Hotel. We were frightened but soon found out that it was the poor wife of one of the men who had been killed that afternoon. She had been with him in the motor car at the time, and was now more or less demented. It was not by any means calculated to soothe our own feelings, but we could do nothing, as the poor girl was well looked after by two ladies who were doctors, Mrs Lyall and another.

Soon after this the Rev Swindell came to our room and said he thought we ought to go onto one of the ships in the Harbour. I said I would rather stay on shore so that I could be on hand in case my husband wanted me, but Mr Swindell said that if Edd had been there he would have been the first to insist that I should go to the ships, and at once too, as that was the best way the women could help, by getting off the Island and so lessening the responsibility of the men and leaving them free to fight.

I said no more about staying on shore, but asked how we could go. Mr Swindell said he would take us in his carriage and put us on a launch. I put poor little Baba into her golf coats and blankets again, and put my own coat and hat on, and Miss Stiles picked up her bag, and Amah ours again, and with Baba in my arms off we set into the night once more.

The drive to Johnson's only took ten minutes. There was a launch waiting, and Mr Swindell put us on it and told the Malay man in charge to take us to the SS *Ipoh*. Two Dutchmen got on just as we moved off. Mr Swindell did not come with us, and out to sea we steamed, the night still as black as ink. We did not know how far we had to go, but in about a quarter of an hour we ranged up alongside the gangway of a ship, which turned out to be the SS *Ipoh*, of the Straits Steamship Company.

As we drew near to the steamer, one of the Dutchmen, the elder of the two, came to me and said "Will you allow me to carry your child up the gangway for you. I am sure you cannot manage to do it." I thanked him very much and said it was kind of him, but that my little girl was only half awake and I was afraid she might cry. He replied "I do not think she will cry with me. I have children of my own, and besides, she is far too heavy for you." By this time we had run alongside the *Ipoh*, so I said to Baba "Let this kind Uncle carry you onto the big steamership" and she just went to him like a lamb, and he carried her on board for me.

All seemed very quiet on board, there did not seem to be anyone about. I took Baba into the saloon and seeing a lady I knew slightly, I said "Do you know if there are any cabins to be had?" She said "I am afraid not, most of the people are lying on mattresses on the deck up above." Just at that moment another lady came up and said "Do put your little girl in the berth in my cabin, my two little children are asleep there, and I can have a long chair." While she was saying this, the lady I knew kept prodding me in the back, so I felt that something was wrong. I thanked the lady therefore and said I would try and find a cabin; I said my child might be restless and disturb hers. She was very pressing, but all the time she was talking my friend kept up a steady poking, so I was firm and refused the offer, and gave Baba into Miss Stiles' charge while I went off to try and find a cabin. It turned out later on that both the children in the cabin had whooping cough, and in two days time the lady herself was down with 'dengue', a kind of influenza and very catching, so we had a lucky escape.

I had not gone far before I met a Chinese boy. I fancy he knew me for I seemed to recognize his face. I asked him if there was a cabin to be had, and he showed me one which he said was the only one left and there was no fan or light in it. However it was a place to put Baba in to sleep, so I gladly took it. I took Baba out of her blanket and put her in the top berth. She sat up, looked round and said "Mummy, where are Charlie and Jackie?" (two little boys who came out with us on the *Mishima Maru*). Then she said "Mummy, where will dear old Daddy sleep?" I had to swallow a big, big lump before I could say "Dear old Daddy will not get any sleep tonight dearie, he is a soldier, but I hope he will get some tomorrow."

Baba then settled down and went off to sleep, and didn't wake until 6.30am. After she was asleep, I told Amah to get into one of the other bunks and go to sleep too, which she did, and Miss Stiles and I found a long chair each, and lay on them all night outside the cabin door.

Never shall I forget the anxiety of that night. Of course we never shut our eyes once, but just lay there quietly, praying for the safety of our men on shore. I did not know where Edd was, but felt he was in the thickest of it all. We did not hear any firing until just as dawn was breaking, and then there was quite a lot of it. At 5.30 we got up from our chairs, and just washed our faces and hands; we did not dare to take off or change any of our clothes (they had dried on us twice during the night), but just tidied up our hair. I can't describe our feelings, they were too much of a jumble, one moment we longed to see the first launch coming out, and the next we dreaded to look for it, in case it might bring us the bad news we were all half expecting to receive.

I felt afraid to ask about Edd when the first man (I believe it was Mr Swindell) did arrive at the ship, but I summoned up my courage at last, and was told that Eddie had gone to Pasir Panjang early the night before and had not been seen since. The news also came that there had been a big fight at Pasir Panjang, and no one knew if anyone, or who, had been killed. Tuesday was indeed a terrible day, but I must leave the further happenings on the ships until another chapter, and let Edd tell what had been going on on shore since we parted.

Falling In

Edwin A. Brown

It is now necessary to go back to the time when I arrived at the Drill Hall that Monday night, and to continue the story from where it left off at the end of the first chapter.

When I had rung up Molly, my first thought was of course for the remnants of my own Company, and I went across to the Chinese Club, which is also Company Headquarters, to find out how many men I could muster. I expected to find only a few men, as nearly all the Company had gone to the islands that morning, and so you can judge my surprise when I found over forty men, some of whose faces I had not seen for years. I recognized them as old ex Volunteers, and it appears that all the ex members rallied during the night. The humorous part is that they all appeared in uniform and, whereas in the European Drill Hall everybody seemed to be snatching any khaki they could lay their hands on, my little lot arrived at their headquarters fully equipped. Where they got their things from I've never found out, but there they were. I collared the Colour Sergeant and two men, and we went over to the Drill Hall, where there was by this time a crowd of all sorts of men, to where Mr St Clair stood charge over the ammunition, and I drew a liberal supply for my detachment and went back and distributed it. Then, getting particulars as to my strength, and telling the men to stand by in case they were wanted, I went back to the Drill Hall. Everything was in semi darkness, outside the road was crowded with motor cars without lights, or with only small ones, road lights were out, and generally the surroundings would even in ordinary cases have given one the blues. In the present instance therefore they did not conduce to our lightheartedness especially as we expected any moment to get news of the mutineers having attacked our outposts.

As I got to the Drill Hall, I met Major Glennie who was in command there, and he asked me to find out how many men there were in the Drill Hall. You must understand that, with the exception of an odd man or two, there were no Volunteers there, they had all moved off some time ago, the place was now full of all sorts of oddments of Europeans, beachcombers, parsons, Engineers, heads of firms, all in dirty clothes without exception, some just as they had come from tennis or golf. I fell them in in two rough lines and got them numbered off. There were about sixty men, and I reported so to Glennie. He said I had better get off with them to the advanced base, which was the P&O Wharf, and when I heard this I was relieved in a way, because it showed that, at all events so far, the mutineers had not got as near to Singapore as we had thought. On the other hand, that wharf is the nearest to the islands where all military stores are kept, and it would be necessary to hold it in order to keep up Communications.

Well, I gave my sixty men the order to move off, and I nearly cried when I saw them try to do it. Not more than half a dozen, I should think, had even seen a rifle before, and as for military movements, I'd already given up any hope that they knew anything about them. So I just told them in plain language what I wanted, "March out to the front of the Drill Hall, you'll see two lorries there, get in, 30 men to a lorry, and keep a seat for me in front of the first," and so we went off. Glennie told me to report to Major Watson RGA who was in charge at the P&O Wharf, hand over the men to him, and then get back to the Drill Hall for further orders. So I gave the order and away we went on our journey to the Wharf.

Of course no trams were running, so our route, which lay along the tram lines, was deserted, and we sped along the dark roads quicker than the old lorries had ever gone in their lives. We heard a couple of shots as we went along, and as a matter of fact, though we did not know it at the time, some mutineers were along a road that ran parallel to the one we were on, but somewhat more inland. All lights were, if not out, very nearly so, and generally speaking one's feelings could not be described as comfortable.

However we got down to the P&O Wharf without mishap, and I reported as ordered to Major Watson, whom I had never seen before, and who didn't know me or who I was. I handed over the men and lorries to him, got into a motor car, and rushed back to the Drill Hall again.

The first thing I did was to see if my own men were alright, by this time Lt Ong Siang had turned up, and they were doing patrol work in the streets outside. Glennie told me he wanted to keep them by him (there were about forty by this time) as he would have to send motor patrols out round the outskirts of the town, and he therefore wished me to take another batch of men down to the P&O Wharf, and report to Major Watson for instruction. This I did, the batch this time being if possible a more shabby-looking lot than before, and we got to the wharf safely. By this time there was quite a crowd of men of all sorts at the wharf, and Watson asked me if it was necessary to go back again. I told him I had instructions to place myself under his orders, and he said I'd better stop there, as the fun would probably start in that direction and, from the look of the men, officers would be badly wanted. He asked if the men I had brought had received ammunition, and I told him that they had only been given 20 rounds apiece at the Drill Hall. (This was the order there, although I had bagged more for my Chinese!) He said "Good God, do they think this is going to be a sham fight? Get them some more at once," so I spent the next half hour or so marching the civilians on to the pitch black wharf, in imminent danger of stumbling over the edge, and loading them up with 100 rounds each. Of course they had nowhere to put it; most men received it in their hats and then distributed it about their person afterwards. Then any amount of the men had of course turned up in white clothes; these were sent up to a bundle, or rather a huge pile, of cast-off khaki uniforms, and told to fit themselves out. They did this by grabbing the first coat and trousers they came to and changing as quickly as possible. There was a nervous tension about them all which didn't allow them to worry about fit or look, but why is it that on such occasions as these each man seems to get exactly the thing that could never by any chance belong to him? Little men got big suits, fat men got thin suits and vice versa, and when they had covered up their whiteness, so to speak, they looked even worse than before.

Then we sat down and waited. My own feelings were not very nice just at this time. Remember that I hadn't the faintest idea what had become of Molly and Baba; the last I had heard of them was when I rang them up in the rush at the Drill Hall, and they had not left the house then. In the meantime the wildest rumours were afloat, and motor cars, arriving every minute, kept bringing fresh news of another murder. Every time one arrived I got to think that I should hear of Molly and Baba being among the number, until I got to hate the sight of an arriving car. At last I could stand it no longer, and having nothing to do but wait, at the moment, I went along to the P&O Pilots' Bungalow, which is on the Wharf, and got through on the telephone to a house near the Chinese Girls' School, and sent a message to see if Molly had arrived there. I got a reply, but unfortunately no news either of Miss Stiles or of Molly, and that made things worse than ever. I went back to my motor car, where I was getting a bit of rest while I could, and there met Price, the Chaplain, who cheered me up a good deal by telling me that he knew that a systematic enquiry was being made for any who by some chance or another had been stranded in the outlying districts. So that Molly had in all probability been taken somewhere if – it was rather a big 'if' at that time – nothing had happened to her first. A few minutes after however, I got a message from a Volunteer on telephone duty that some lady – he mentioned her name but I did not know it, and have never remembered it since – had rung up to say that Mrs Brown and party had got to Raffles Hotel. I'm sorry I never could remember the lady's name, as I should very much like to have thanked her, later on, for her trouble. It was certainly the most welcome telephone message I have ever had.

By this time it must have been after 11 o'clock, and with the lifting of my anxiety, hunger began to assert itself. I therefore thought that some food would be a good thing, and had a look round, but there was nothing at all to be had. Kennedy the ASC Lieutenant was very busy sending off loads of bully beef and Aerated Water to the various columns and outposts, but he had completely forgotten the hundred odd men directly under his view at the P&O Wharf. I drew his attention to the matter and gently suggested that we should be fed too, and he nearly had a fit. A message was at once sent off to the depot for food for us, and then we sat down to wait once more.

All at once there seemed to be signs of something about to happen. Men began running here and there in the little room where the telephone line was – the only place where a light was allowed – and then in the middle up dashed the motor lorry with food for us, bully beef packed in strong cases.

I had previously lined the men up – there were about 70 "dug-ups" – to receive their share of food in an orderly manner, and we were busy trying to open a strong case with a bayonet, when Major Watson came out of the little room with a paper in his hand, calling for me. I answered him, and he thrust the paper in my hand and told me to read it. It ran "Seven hundred mutineers preparing to advance on Singapore from Alexandra. Warn Col Brownlow at once and reinforce him." Nice news, wasn't it? And all Watson could spare was about twenty-five dug-ups and about fifteen details of APD, ASC, RE, and RGA. With this little and by no means brilliant force I was ordered to "push off like Hell" to Col Brownlow at the junction of Pasir Panjang and Alexandra Road, the nearest point occupied by us to the mutineers' barracks.

I shoved my men into cars, six men to a car, jumped into the first myself, and told the rest to follow me, and we were off, leaving the unopened case of Beef lying on the wharf. It's astonishing what fools there are in the world, but at least three of those motors turned in the opposite direction to me on getting out of the P&O gates, and I had to stop the column and send a motor back to fetch them.

Then we were off again, through the pitch darkness – there was no moon at all – obeying our instructions as to driving, quite literally, until we got somewhere near to the crossroads where I slowed up. All of a sudden a voice came out of the darkness, "Halt, who's there?" I pulled up at once, and then the voice came again, "Put those lights out," as the few small lights we had on the cars had to be extinguished.

When I had satisfied the sentry as to who we were, we were allowed to proceed slowly, and now after passing another sentry post, we could make out forms of men sitting or lying on the ground, some sailors, some in khaki. We went on until we saw motor cars looming up in front of us, and we pulled up behind them. I left my men to tumble out by themselves and went in search of Col Brownlow.

We had arrived!!

Engaging the Enemy

Edwin A. Brown

I found Col Brownlow with Lt Olliver, The GSO (acting) [General Staff Officer (acting)], in a Chinese hut at the corner of Alexandra Road and Pasir Panjang Road. By the light of a smoky oil lamp he read my message. There seemed to be a lot of doubt about the truth of it, and if it had been verbal I'm afraid I should not have been believed, but fortunately it was a written message as well, and as its source was Government House, where the Headquarters had taken up their abode, it was impossible to question it.

But you may imagine what it felt like to know that somewhere, certainly not more than a mile off, behind that line of mangrove swamp and bits of scrub, seven hundred men well trained in the use of arms were concentrating, and all we had were about 200 men, 90 of whom were sailors, about 70 Volunteers, 50 of whom had never been on the Range at this time, and the remainder were my men, most of whom had never had a rifle in their hands before, of which they gave ample proof later on, as you shall hear.

But we had one great asset that was denied to the mutineers, we had Col Brownlow himself. He had spent most of his military life on the North West frontier of India, and whereas an amateur – who under the circumstances of the times might easily have been in charge – would have followed drill-book rules and taken up a defensive position, thereby no doubt giving the enemy time to arrange the method of their attack, Col Brownlow decided to attack himself, even with what seemed a totally inadequate force, so as not to give the odds time to increase against him. Besides there was Col Martin and the men of the MSVR in the Colonel's bungalow to be relieved, and as they had no food or water, that would have to be taken in hand at once.

It takes very much longer to write this than it took Col Brownlow to make up his mind. He turned to me, saying he was glad to see me, and asked me to bring my Chinese Company along to the van, for, to use his own words, "They're the only trained infantry in the place now". I told him that the Company was all over at the islands, and that all I'd got were about 40 odds and ends, was rather pathetic under the circumstances, for the sight of me had given him cause to expect a reinforcement of at least 100 trained men.

However his decision to attack in the early morning was unaltered, and so he sent us all off to get a bit of rest before we had to be on the move again. I groped my way back to the rear, and found my collection, keeping in a lump fortunately, but with no order among them at all. The details from the Services had certainly fallen in, but the rest were, as the Americans say, 'jest standin' aroun'. I can think of no better expression for them. It was almost too dark to see them at all, and as there would be no more light, and not as much time, when we should have to get a move on, I had to devise some kind of scheme for handling them. So I got the civilians into some kind of order and counted them, finding I had just thirty. I had also ten details. Then the idea came. Why not give three 'dug-ups' to each army man to father and shepherd and generally look after, with threats of untold penalties if they lost anyone? A great scheme, promptly acted on, greatly to the amusement of the sailors standing near. That the idea of the scheme was upset later on by one in greater authority than myself is beside the point, the effect of it lasted long enough to get the men quietly into motor cars for a rest, and gather them in the morning. That it evidently served another useful purpose, namely gave them some amusement, is proved by a little incident that happened later, and for that reason alone I can take credit to myself.

You must remember that none of us had ever heard a shot fired in anger before. The night was so black that even at this time I had not recognized a single face among my men (although it turned out afterwards that I had several friends among them). On the right of the road was swamp and scrub, on the left a bit of grassland rising to a small hill. Only occasionally the stillness was broken by a shot from the outposts, and across the sky stretched two narrow beams of light, the searchlights from Pulo Brani fixed on Col Martin's bungalow. Is it to be wondered that there was a danger of men getting 'the wind up'? I say without fear of being laughed at that it was just the rottenest four hours I ever spent, and it was my own scheme of arrangement of my men that actually gave me the diversion I needed, as you shall hear.

I had put my men into the cars, with instructions to get what rest they could, and I then began to look about for a place for myself. It had by this time got very cold, and as I had nothing on but a pair of shorts and a thin shirt, I was not feeling at all comfortable. I was standing by one of my motors at the time, and it looked as if there might be room for me on the front seat, so, with a "Any room for a little one?" I climbed in. I found myself next a private of the Royal Engineers, one of my odds and ends, and he was chuckling away to himself like anything. After a time I asked him what the matter was, and in broad cockney he delivered himself somewhat after this fashion. "That's a funny bloke what's in charge of us; fancy me in charge of three men! That there bloke didn't know what 'e was doin' of! Strike me, someone 'll be makin' me a bloomin' Major General next!" And on he went, chuckling to himself, and evidently ruminating on the vicissitudes of life. He little thought that the 'funny bloke', as he called him, was sitting as close as he could get to him for warmth, and you may be sure I didn't enlighten him. Remember it was so dark we couldn't see each other's faces, and there was nothing to distinguish us in our dress.

Bye the bye, this darkness was useful in one way, because it did not allow me to find out that exactly alongside my car, at the side of the road, were the bodies of two mutineers lying where they had fallen, shot earlier in the afternoon!! It would have considerably spoilt what little of comfort there was in that night's rest, had I been aware of these gruesome reminders of the day's happenings. It still seemed to be as dark as ever when the word came down the column that it was time to tumble out. So out we got, and stretched our stiffened and cramped limbs. If you ever have occasion to spend a night in a small Ford car with five other full grown men, and also with rifles, you'll know how we felt that morning, but as a matter of mere curiousity I don't advise you to try it.

The call then came for Officers, and having by this time got my men into some kind of order, I went along to the junction of the roads. By this time daylight was beginning to come, and I found Col Brownlow sitting on a stone coping over the roadside drain, smoking a cigarette and looking supremely happy. His wife told me afterwards that he simply loved expeditions of this kind. Hating his office stool like poison, the old man was in his element in the field, and if the adventure was a little more uncertain than usual, the more he was pleased. With him was his dog, a wire haired fox terrier, which I believe was about to experience his twenty-eighth engagement!!

The objective of the morning was Col Martin's bungalow where, as I have already told you, Col Martin, some officers and their wives, and the officers and men of the MSVR were besieged. Between where we were and the bungalow lay the greater part of the Native Barracks, the plan of the ground being something like this:

<u>Key</u>
1 Water cistern
2 Quarter guard
3 Colonel Martin's bungalow
4 Officer's mess
5 Sandpit

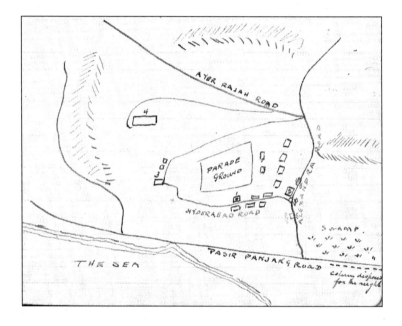

ABOVE Original sketch by Edwin A. Brown.
OPPOSITE Edwin A. Brown's map with transcribed names.

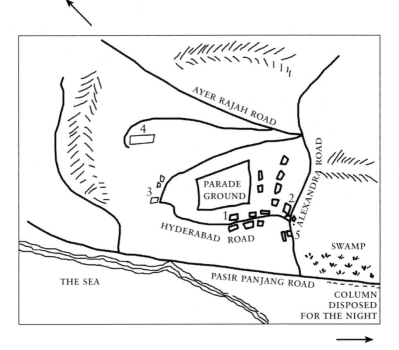

PRESENT-DAY AYER RAJAH
EXPRESSWAY (AYE) TO NATIONAL
UNIVERSITY OF SINGAPORE

AYER RAJAH ROAD

4

PARADE
GROUND

ALEXANDRA ROAD

3

1

2

5

HYDERABAD ROAD

THE SEA

PASIR PANJANG ROAD

SWAMP

COLUMN
DISPOSED
FOR THE NIGHT

PRESENT-DAY
TELOK BLANGAH ROAD
TO VIVO CITY / SENTOSA

Col Brownlow explained to us that the information he had received from his outposts showed that the range of hills on the right of Alexandra Road was occupied by the mutineers, and that he would endeavour to clear them off there first, then swing to his left and drive them all back upon the bungalow, where he hoped they would be caught between two fires, and generally be messed up. The sailors were to form the advance guard, with the Volunteers, Rifles and Marines in the centre, while the nondescript body under me was told off for the rearguard. With us, or rather partly with us and with the centre or main body, was a lorry with a Naval Gatling Gun and crew. It did not take Col Brownlow very long to tell us what he wanted doing, and to me, after the amateur efforts of field days, it was quite a treat to notice the ease of his remarks, and the few words he took to make everything perfectly understandable. Some of the flank picquets, sent out over night, were now called in, and I was joined by several dirty looking objects in one of which, dressed in tennis shoes, a slouch hat, an old suit of khaki obviously not his own, and with a tennis towel round his neck, I was glad to recognize Lt Kemp of the Volunteer Engineers, my old friend and shooting companion. He attached himself to me as a volunteer. I had no command to give him, because previous to his arrival Col Brownlow had come along to inspect my noble band, and seeing some

Regulars among them, had promptly bagged the lot and sent them on to swell the main body. So away went my pleasant scheme for handling my men!! I told the Colonel and he laughed, but he said I would easily find someone to help me. He wanted to know who I had, and I couldn't tell him, for up till that time it had been too dark to recognize faces. Now I was glad to see some old friends, and one, a lawyer living near me, was on my suggestion appointed my Lieutenant by the Colonel – the only case of promotion on the field of battle that Singapore can lay claim to!! Everyone laughed, but Cooke Yarborough was fearfully bucked about it. He had a white topee on, and – men do funny things when they are excited – the first thing he did was to go full length on the road and rub his topee in the drain, to get it the colour of khaki, as he said. It looked when he had finished like an early example of camouflaging, a word that at that time we had not heard of.

Then the Colonel asked for two intelligent men for runners, and I picked him out Cameron and Talma. The brother of the former had been killed earlier in the afternoon but he did not know it at this time, and Talma was an athlete and suitable for the job. Both men, by the way, were run to a standstill before the morning was out, and I found them later on sitting on the roadside trying to get their wind back and absolutely finished. So Kemp could have no command in theory, but practically of course he was of great help.

Then we started. The Navy swung past up Alexandra Road, soon followed by the Rifles and the Marines. Then came the lorry with the Gatling Gun and then us. We had only got about 100 yards up the road when brisk firing broke out ahead of us, and we could see the Navy boys extending through the scrub on the right of the road, and occasional puffs of smoke from the top of the ridge, where the mutineers were. For safety's sake, as we were well within range of stray bullets, I sent my men into the ditches on either side of the road, to walk along in them instead of along the middle of the road. But after all it was not so much the enemy's fire that was the danger, but my own men. One of them, feeling that the time for terrible battle had been thrust upon him, so to speak, at last been forcibly thrust upon him, decided that he had better be fully prepared. He therefore proceeded to load his rifle. Having pulled open the breech – I don't think he had ever had a service rifle in his hand before – he inserted a cartridge in the chamber, and then closed the breech again. He was surprised to find something (the cocking piece, although he didn't know it) sticking out of the end, a position it certainly hadn't occupied before!! "This must be put right again," thought he, "or I shall be found out." Whereat, just as a preliminary to further effort, he pulled the trigger!! Now Kemp and I were walking in the middle of the road, talking and gauging the distance of the ridge from where we were, when there was a 'bang' almost in our right ears, a scatter of gravel about six inches in front of our toes, and simultaneously a yell from the ditch on the left, and a man danced up to us waving his arms and shouting "I'm wounded, I'm wounded." He seemed extraordinarily pleased with himself, seemed in fact to take the thing rather as an honour than otherwise. Sure enough, the bullet had caught his shoulder, torn away the coat, and grazed the flesh. I sent him back to the corner of the roads where the advanced dressing station was, because in this climate even flesh wounds, if not promptly attended to, might prove serious, and then I let the perpetrator of the deed have it!! Have you ever heard me swear? There are occasions when a good flow of language is necessary, and this was one of them. The thing that made us extra angry was the foolishness of the idiot for pointing his rifle into the middle of the road where we were walking instead of into the scrub on his right. I insisted on examining rifles then and there, and finding several loaded, had them unloaded again. And so we went on, with all rifles unloaded, into the action that was proceeding on our front. It sounds curious now I am writing this, to say that we were safer with our rifles unloaded than with them ready for action, but so it was.

There was of course no time to explain about magazines, cut-offs and safety catches, those ordinary means of safety had to be eliminated from our consideration.

Shortly after this the move to the left took place, as the Navy had succeeded in their work of pushing the mutineers off Arab Hill, the name of the hill on the right of the road. And that meant that it was now our time to take a hand in the game. We were passing a small sandpit at the time, I remember, and up the slope at the back of it was a long cast iron building with some barrack storerooms behind it. It was a good place to start off from, so up we went, scrambling up the edge of the pit and getting into the corrugated latrine, where we had told the men to collect and wait for further orders. Just as I got inside a bullet hit the place. Looking back upon it now, I cannot help laughing. The noise made was of course something terrific, for the empty iron building simply lent itself to echoes, but the different ways it affected the men was the humourous part. Some took no notice, but most, I think, thought that they were in heavy action at last. Some even went the length of lying down and pushing their rifles out of the door we'd come in by – the wrong direction!!

It was here that one of the men came up to me in great excitement, holding out his rifle by the barrel. "Here, what's wrong with this?" he said. I looked at it, and in disgust answered "You silly ass, you've lost the bolt". "The bolt," he replied, "what's that?" It was no use going into technicalities, and any simple answer would do, so I merely replied "Oh, the thing you push the cartridges in with." "Yes", he said, "now you mention it, I did hear something drop", in quite a calm resigned voice, as if it was unfortunate, but didn't really matter!! I reflected that he might be safer with the rifle as it was, but nevertheless told him to take my rifle – I had picked one up at the Drill Hall – and leave his old one in the shed.

Then I went out to have a look round, and really to let the men see that the battle had not begun as far as we were concerned. It was time to push on also, as I could hear that our right was again engaged. And here I did try a little exhortation, mainly to exhort the men to exercise their powers of mimicry and follow my movements as much as possible. I didn't want them to expose themselves more than possible, as we might come under fire at any moment. Then off we went in single file, I leading, to get onto Hyderabad Road.

We had to cross the Horse lines, and just as we were preparing to rush – no cover here of course – we saw a movement in the jungle at the side, and about fifty Indians came out, with their hands above their heads. It turned out afterwards that these were part of the loyal ones who had taken cover in the jungle the night before, but that we didn't of course know at the time. In the meantime, I was saddled with a lot of prisoners which I didn't want. However it couldn't be helped, and fortunately a temporary prison was at hand in the shape of a barrack room. So I bundled the lot in there, and left some of the older men, who were showing signs of fatigue, in charge, pushing on with my somewhat reduced force.

We were now among the barracks proper, and had to go very cannily, for bullets were flying about, although we could see no enemy. Every building had to be examined, and it was exciting work, because at any moment we might have come across one in which some of the enemy was lurking. I also was unarmed now, and therefore somewhat at a disadvantage.

However, in one of the huts I had a find. A Rifle, with chamber and magazine loaded, and 150 rounds of ammunition in a haversack, both rifle and haversack stamped "Malay State Guides"!!! So some at least of the MSG sided with the mutineers. However he'd run away evidently – perhaps he'd already surrendered to me, unarmed, and his little lot of property came in very handy, I can assure you.

We picked up a few more surrendering men and sent them back to our prison, and crept on along the drain on the right of the road. Bullets were now flying in profusion down the centre, but owing to a high bank we were under cover. I was making for a big concrete erection, a water cistern, and knew that we should not get past there without getting the fire down, as beyond it there was no cover. It was here we came across Col Brownlow, very relieved indeed to see me, and very exercised in his mind as to whether I would come up here, or remain, according to Drill Book, as rearguard!! His flank here was very badly exposed, and an attack would have meant the taking of his front in the flank, and a consequent retirement if not worse. However, I was there, and it seemed just in time too, for the fire was increasing in intensity, and so far, of course, had not been answered.

Col Brownlow told me to hang on there as long as possible if the line didn't go forward, and if it did to advance with it, and then left me to my own devices. The first thing to do was to guard my own left flank by occupying the buildings across the road. It was pretty dangerous work crossing that road, but I got one or two men across with instructions to make cover for themselves on the verandah in the rear, and then I turned my attention to getting the mastery of the fire that was being poured upon us. I instructed as well as I could some men in the art of creeping forward, and then sent them off up the little slope behind the cistern, to get into position and to open a counter fire at once. It was really pitiable to watch them. They had only perhaps a dozen yards to go, but their ideas of cover were nil, and in that short distance three of them were hit, one through the groin, and he rolled down into the ditch to my very feet, in terrible agony. Fortunately the RAMC were not far away, with Capt Fraser, the doctor, and they soon took charge of our wounded. I do not think there need have been these casualties if only the men had had some knowledge of the way to advance under fire.

Here, in the midst of the tragedy, the comic side appeared of course. I remember being at this time considerably startled by a sound as of a small avalanche above my head, and looking up I saw a British officer, arms spreadeagled, revolver in one hand and stick in the other, falling to earth – where he duly came with a mighty bump – as it were from the clouds. It appears that Col Brownlow had sent a few men to reinforce me, under this officer, and he had come along gaily enough under cover as he thought, when, reaching a tree, he looked up, and there in the branches sat a mutineer with his rifle pointed downwards, calmly taking aim at him and about to pull the trigger!! I don't know where the bullet went, but from all accounts that officer jumped much faster than the bullet could travel, and to such a purpose that his jump carried him over the little hill at the side of the road – which by the way he didn't know was so near – with the result that he came sailing through the air in the graceful manner mentioned, to be deposited full length at my feet in the ditch.

Immediately after, shots rang out from the houses across the road, and I took a chance and dashed across to see what was happening. I found some very excited civilians, one especially so, who rushed up shouting "I got him, sir, I got him", and evidently thinking that the mutiny was now quelled for good and all. After suggesting to him that if he didn't lie down the boot would be on the other leg, I looked about me, and sure enough the proof of the man's remark lay about twenty yards away, just outside the line of scrub, in the shape of a dead mutineer. It seems that some of them had got the idea of creeping up and getting into those houses on my flank. However, unluckily for them, I had had the idea first, and very luckily for us, I may say. Seeing the houses occupied they had retreated into the undergrowth again, leaving one of their number dead.

It was now necessary that we should be more active. The firing was increasing in intensity all along the front, and it sounded as if the climax was not far off. I therefore extended my men as well as I could from the cistern, across the road, under the houses etc, wherever they could get an advantageous spot. While doing this, a party of Volunteers rushed across from the centre direction and established themselves, with great excitement, in my rear. I'm not quite sure what they gave as their reason, but I believe the officer in charge said something about protecting the retirement!! You must know that rearguard actions are about the only thing ever practiced by the Volunteers here, I suppose those in charge have a feeling that it is a tactic that will be used more than any other in an emergency. However, on this occasion the gallant officer in charge of this band was not going to be allowed to put his knowledge to the test, if in any way I could prevent it. I'm afraid I used some more language that was more forcible than polite, and annexed the batch of men with that officer!! I don't know what happened to him, he seemed to fade away, which was just as well, as he was my senior!! I blame him still for nearly having me shot. Up to that time I'd been making careful use of cover, but I suppose I forgot, for in my 'argument' with his men, I stood up by one of the houses, and immediately there was a 'ping' and a noise like a hammer striking just above my head. I went down to cover again, but I found out after that about one inch separated the top of my helmet from the course of that bullet. It really wasn't a bad shot considering that it was a 'snap', the man couldn't have had time to aim.

My men were now pouring a steady fire along the road

towards the slight bend (marked with an X in the previous sketch). We couldn't see any enemy, but our object was to help to get the fire under to enable an advance to be made. And shortly after, the time came, for from far on the right a roar started; a roar that once heard can never be mistaken, the sound of British sailors cheering. Down the line it came, that unmistakable British battlecry. There was no need for any command, my men, and I myself, picked up that shout, and as we joined in it jumped to our feet and rushed, a shouting cheering mass, with no order, simply intent on getting forward and finishing the job. We mingled with the sailors and the Volunteers, all well up in the charge, and every moment expected to hear an answering charge from the Bungalow. But alas no such thing occurred. For some reason or other, never actually fathomed, those 80 to 100 men remained 'doggo' in the bungalow, and allowed three to four hundred mutineers to stream past on either side, and to get away into the thick country at the back. I think Col Brownlow could have cried. He had managed his part of the business so well, and when he saw his men going forward in that final charge must have had visions of rounding up all the mutineers in one fell swoop, and it must have been terribly hard for him to see the indecision of the men in the house. In extenuation it must be admitted that the shock of the mutiny had been too much for poor Col Martin, and he could not at that time have been responsible for his actions, but it seems queer that it struck no-one to get out of that house with a bayonet in front of him, and get to business!! Why, they could almost have jumped on the mutineers from the house verandahs.

Well, there we were at last, a sweating breathless lot of human beings, and it looked as if there was nothing more to be done but go back again!! In the meantime I began to remember that from tiffin the day before I hadn't had a morsel to eat or drink except the sandwich Mary made for me before I left the house. It was now well past ten o'clock, and as there was a lot of confusion around the house, I thought that a quick forage on my own account would not be noticed! But foraging wasn't much use in that house! Eighty men had been there all night, and had cleaned the place out of everything eatable and especially drinkable. I was just going away despondent when I saw a milk tin thrown in the corner of a room. On the principle of not missing a chance I picked it up and found that it was unopened!! Joy!! I picked up a bayonet – there were lots lying about – and was making the necessary holes in the tin, when who should pop his head into the room but Col Brownlow himself, I believe engaged upon the same pursuit as I was!! So we shared that milk tin between us, and as far as I can find out, no-one else got anything, or even thought about it!!

Milk finished, Col Brownlow sent for the senior officers, and I was pushing off to collect my men when he turned to me and said he particularly wanted me to stay. So I was present – the only one not directly concerned – when Col Martin and Col Derrick (of the Volunteers) got the rough edge of Brownlow's tongue for about ten minutes. I don't know what Derrick had done to rouse the old man's ire, but he started answering back. Whew, didn't he just get it. I couldn't help laughing to myself at the difference between this peppery full vocabularied Colonel and the mild little gentleman seen so regularly at Service in the Cathedral on Sundays. But the thought of those mutineers streaming away over the country, and of the work it would take to round them up, was enough to reduce milder men than the Colonel to a state of frenzy.

Well the explosion ceased at length, and the Colonel was himself again. He decided that he couldn't hold the bungalow, for he had with him all the available forces in Singapore, and they might be wanted elsewhere at any moment. So a retirement was decided on, and then he turned to me and said he'd kept me by him as he wanted me to take charge of all prisoners etc on the way back. Sounds easy, doesn't it, now that one writes about it on paper? But if you had seen that bungalow you would have food for thought. There must have been at least fifty rifles and bayonets lying about all over the floors. I called up as many of my men as I could find and with Kemp's assistance we got to work. Buckets were produced, and the bolts of the rifles were taken out and put in the buckets. We had to do this ourselves, my men didn't know how.

Seeing some Indians standing near, I concluded that they were men who had given themselves up, and accordingly 'took possession' of them as part of my bag of prisoners. I began to load them up with the boltless rifles, to their intense disgust, but I had to get my rifles away somehow, and soon they were hung about with eight or twelve rifles apiece. I found out afterwards that they were Native officers, loyal men who had taken refuge with the Colonel when the mutiny broke out. No wonder they were disgusted at being used as beasts of burden!

By this time the retirement had begun, and there was a general movement towards the quarter guard, which was the concentrating point. By this time my force had dwindled to about ten men, some had been wounded, others were winded, some had lost themselves or got mixed up with other units, in any case I couldn't find them. I got hold of a section of MSVR, to act as a rear cover for me, for by this time my small force had all its work cut out to guard the prisoners, and in addition we had to bring in with us the

40 odd mules belonging to the MSG Battery. Now mules at the best of times are contrary animals, so we decided to relieve ourselves of some of our responsibility by letting 40 prisoners take care of them. One man one mule, and I don't know to this day whether the men looked after the mules or the mules after the men. Certain it is that one mule at all events had no use for a mutineer, for he gave one look at his keeper, and then lifted him clear into the drain! However no bones were broken, and the punishment fitted the crime quite nicely!

As we were concentrating we were fired on again, and my MSVR Section opened out and skirmished through some very long grass to clear up any possible ambush. All of a sudden two men got up within five yards of each other; one an MSVR, the other a mutineer. Both rifles seemed to go off together, but I'm thankful to say the mutineer missed, and received the bullet of my man in his head. Another man was seen running away and was shot. Just two snipers and nothing else.

So in time we got away, and by this time you may be sure we were very tired. The excitement had finished and it was all we could do to keep ourselves alert and prevent straggling. A long line we were too along the road, forty mules and their attendant mutineers, about fifty other prisoners marching in fours, and my few men dotted along the line with orders to shoot any man who made a bolt for it.

But we got into the end of the town at last, with only one more bit of excitement, a bit of sniping from one of the hills on Keppel Golf Course, and at length the halt was sounded, and we knew that the end of that episode had come at last. The problem, however, of what to do with the mules and prisoners had still to be faced.

Col Brownlow came up to me and discussed the matter. As far as the mules were concerned, there was a nice place ready to hand in the enclosed Compound of the Police Station, opposite which we had halted, and we quickly pushed the animals in there, and were thankful to see the last of them. Col Brownlow had an idea of shoving the prisoners in along with them, but this would have necessitated a large guard being left on duty, and as everyone was dog-tired and done up, it was finally decided that I should take some motor lorries, load up with prisoners, and hand them over to the Authorities at the Gaol.

I proceeded to collect my two lorries and commandeer some motor cars. I divided my men up as well as I could – I had only about 10, with Cooke Yarborough and Kemp – and I filled the lorries with the prisoners. I got Capt Hall of the 5th LI to come with me as an interpreter, and after impressing on the Indians the fact that if one of them dared to stand up, even to move his position, he would be shot at sight by the guards on the lorries, we started. First went a motor car with a couple of men sitting on the back, then the two lorries, and finally another car with Kemp, Yarborough, Hall and myself. We arrived safely at the open space in front of the Gaol, and after taking due precautions in case of an attempted escape by the prisoners, we went to the door of the prison and knocked. No answer, all was silent and still. We knocked again, this time with the butt of a rifle. Still no answer but distinct sounds of habitation and a lot of shuffling. We raised our voices and finally, after a long delay, a muffled voice replied "Who's there?". "Officers with prisoners," we answered. "What officers?" was asked. "Capt Brown" I replied. "Don't know you" the voice came back.

That was a bit of a poser, but I informed the gentleman behind the door that I had ninety prisoners and a guard of ten and I wasn't going to stand there all day for him! Apparently however he thought different, for "Don't know you" was all the answer we could get. Then Hall had a try, and after him Kemp, but only the same answer came back, "Don't know you". By this time our tempers, none the better for what we had been through, and our tiredness, were getting very strained, and I invited Cooke Yarborough to put his face to the keyhole; perhaps they would recognize his nose – a prominent feature.

The mention of 'Cookie' seemed to give the doubting gentleman within some confidence, for 'Cookie' is a well known lawyer here, and a grill was opened high up in the door and a face appeared. The view obtained seemed to satisfy him, for immediate activity with bolts and bars started, and finally the big doors swung inwards and revealed to our gaze a most astonishing sight! "For God's sake put those things down", we yelled, and at the same time ducked and dodged behind the gateposts, for this was the wonderful picture that met our view. Stretching from one side of the gateway to the other was a row of white clad warders, kneeling, with rifles at the old 'prepare to receive cavalry' position. Behind them, standing, was another row, with revolvers levelled at arms length, and all pointing at us!! Behind, on biscuit boxes, packing cases, and any old thing that happened to be handy, appeared the rest of the personnel of the gaol, natives all, with hatchets, choppers, knives and any old thing they had been able to lay their hands on. In front of all was the chief warder, an old white haired man, and by his side Codrington, the Governor of the Gaol, rather shaky at the knees and holding in his hand a paper, probably the Riot Act, though I never enquired. The whole effect was most dramatic, but shriekingly funny to us, as we begged them to put their guns away in case any of them should go off.

Well we got the gateway cleared at last, and drove the motor lorries into the Courtyard, hurried out the prisoners and made them sit down in rows. I then considered my work over; I had safely delivered the 90 men into the hands of the Gaol authorities, and the exertions and the excitement of the last sixteen to twenty hours were beginning to tell heavily. Food and a wash loomed up very importantly, and so we said farewell to the Gaol, dismissed the motor lorries, and taking the three motor cars and our few guards with us, we drove away to the Drill Hall. There I handed over my men to the Commandant and begged for leave to feed. We got it, and Kemp, Cooke Yarborough, Hall and myself went off to the Club, where we indulged in a bath and a big tiffin. Dirty clothes had to be put on again of course, but we felt more like ourselves after we had eaten.

And then back to the Drill Hall, to more work that must be recounted in another chapter.

And so ended the first phase of the mutiny. The mutineers had been dispersed as a regiment, and there was no further fear of fully organized effort against us. The action of Col Brownlow in attacking as he did, even with the small untrained force at his command, still seems to me, looking back after this lapse of time, to be the real factor that saved Singapore from very serious trouble. Had he given the mutineers time to perfect their arrangements and attack him, there is no doubt that they could easily have overwhelmed us, and would then have had the town at their mercy.

Recently arrived in the East, a 24-year-old Edwin A. Brown
poses for a studio portrait, Singapore 1902.

Mary Brown displays her engagement
ring, 1908.

Edwin A. Brown with his bride Mary,
Singapore 1910.

Edwin, Mary and Barbara Brown shortly before the mutiny,
Singapore 1914.

Mary and Barbara Brown with syce and trap, Singapore.

Burnsall in Rochalie Avenue, the Singapore home of
Edwin and Mary Brown from 1910 to 1924.

Mary and Barbara Brown with syce and family at Burnsall.

Mary and Barbara Brown with
friend at Burnsall, Rochalie Avenue.

Barbara (taller child) and her younger sister Shelagh with their *amahs*.

Chapter I.

Chinese New Year 1915, will long be remembered in the Straits Settlements. As usual at that time of the year, general holidays had been proclaimed, and the godowns were for the most part shut. My company of Volunteers, the Chinese, had been given thirty hours leave from duty — they were doing guards at various points on the island — and on the Monday morning, the 15th, I remobilized ninety two men, and accompanied them to Johnson's Pier, from which point they left by launch for the Islands of Pulo Brani & Blakan Mati, for guard duty.

After getting this business over, & seeing the men safely off, Mary & Miss Stiles, who had been down to see the Company fall in, & myself, left for home again, had a tiffin, and went to our rooms for a "lie-off", having arranged to go for a good walk when the heat of the day was over.

Page one of the original document penned by Edwin A. Brown.

THE SINGAPORE MUTINY.

MANCHESTER MAN'S GALLANTRY.

In the suppression of the mutiny of the 5th Light Infantry (Indian army) at Singapore on February 16 Captain E. A. Brown, of the Chinese Company, Singapore Volunteer Corps, rendered valuable service and received high praise in Lieutenant Colonel Brownlow's report to Headquarters. Captain Brown is a Manchester man and was educated at the Hulme Grammar School. He went out to Singapore in 1900 as the representative of Messrs. Hiltermann, and has taken a leading part in the social life of the colony.

On February 15 a party of British officers and some loyal Malay volunteers were besieged in the Alexandra Barracks by the mutineers, and Lieutenant Colonel Brownlow, R.G.A., advanced to their relief with a small force, which, besides marines and Royal Garrison Artillery men, included 50 volunteers of a recently formed rifle corps and 25 armed civilians, mostly untrained. The last were placed under Captain Brown's command, and with the R.G.A. men formed the reserve. At one point in the attack on the mutineers the reserve were under a very heavy fire, but showed great bravery and by their firm stand averted the failure of the whole operation.

In bringing the services of officers to the notice of Headquarters Lieutenant Colonel Brownlow says:—" Captain Brown, who took charge of the reserve, showed himself to be an exceptionally capable and valuable officer. He was in command of the untrained troops in a very hot little piece of fighting, and but for his good and cool leading it is quite possible that his command might have had to retire, thus disorganising and delaying the whole operation." Captain Brown's name is also mentioned in the report to the War Office recently issued by the Press Bureau.

Edwin A. Brown's gallantry was reported in the *Manchester Guardian* (21.4.1915), the forerunner to *The Guardian*.

LEFT Captain Edwin A. Brown, officer commanding the Chinese Company, Singapore Volunteer Corps, Singapore 1915.

BELOW Singapore Volunteer Corps. Edwin A. Brown under white patch (head obscured). Song Ong Siang to his left.

OPPOSITE Mutineers face the firing squad. [Courtesy Whitaker Family and Imperial War Museum, London]

Honorary Choirmaster of St Andrew's Cathedral,
the founder of both the Singapore Musical
Society and the Children's Orchestra, a respected
businessman, a municipal commissioner, the Chief
Commissioner of Scouts for Singapore and a Justice
of the Peace, Edwin A. Brown would become one of
prewar Singapore's most prominent figures.

Fire at Sea

Mary Brown

Tuesday, the second day of the mutiny, very slowly passed, several men came out to the *Ipoh* to see their wives, all brought different tales of what was going on on shore, none of them had seen or heard anything of Edd. I was thankful beyond words to have Baba with me, and we just played games with nothing. None of the ladies had any needlework or books, nothing to occupy themselves with, neither had the children any toys to play with, but the dear wee things were so good, and there was never a whimper all day.

One lady said to me on this second day "I think all you mothers deserve a prize, you are just splendid, I can't think how you have all managed to keep your children so good and quiet, and you are all dead beat and anxious beyond words."

It was not easy to keep a smiling face and play silly games, but one did not want the chicks to be miserable. Capt Daly was most kind, and did everything in his power to make us comfortable. Most of the ladies were sleeping on deck on mattresses, and about five or six were sharing a cabin to dress and undress in, but as we were all ladies on board we were able partly to dress on deck. We shared hairbrushes, soap etc, and got the men who came off to buy toothbrushes for us. I don't think anybody got a bath that day; Amah managed to get a little hot water and gave Baba as good a bath as could be managed under the circumstances. The ladies looked terribly bedraggled; we were most of us in white skirts and blouses. As a rule we wear a white skirt and blouse for about two hours and then condemn it to the dirty linen basket, so it can be imagined how humbled we looked. Our muslin blouses had been wet through several times and had dried on us, but we were all more or less in the same state, and we were too worried and anxious to care much about how we looked, and oh, we were all so tired out, what with the shock of the night before, the absence of sleep, and the heat of the boat. But everyone seemed too restless to try and lie-off . Every launch that came I hoped against hope to see Eddie on it, and at 3.30pm that day he actually did come, and I could hardly believe my eyes when I saw him.

Baba and I were on the upper deck when we saw the launch coming alongside, and when I told Baba that Daddy had come she did not say anything until we got to the top of the stairs, then she paused, and turning round to all the people who were sitting about, said in a loud voice with a wave of her hand "My Daddy". It was so sweet; and then she turned to me and said "Come on Mummy", and we nearly fell down the stairs in our excitement.

Edd was pretty well fagged out, and so dirty. He had had practically nothing to eat, and no sleep, and said he would give anything for a cup of tea, which I managed to get for him after much talking to the boys, which took up several minutes of the ten he had to stay. I then tried to get a little quiet talk with him in the saloon but it was hopeless, everyone simply swarmed round him, all asking questions at once. We could not go to our cabin and have a quiet time there, as Miss Stiles was dressing in it. At the end of ten minutes Edd said "Well I must go now Molly. I don't know when I shall be out again, but I'll slip across as soon as I get a chance", and soon he was steaming away in the launch, and we were left to carry on the monotonous round of our life once more.

Wednesday and Thursday passed without anything exciting happening; I neither said nor heard anything of Edd, on Thursday people were saying that some of the Volunteers were missing, and I had five different tales told me about Edd on Thursday, and by evening I suppose I got rather jumpy for I felt quite sure he was one of those that were missing and that no-one liked to tell me. Perhaps he was wounded and lying alone in the jungle. It was silly of me, but very real at the time. I couldn't sleep that night, and all Friday I was very anxious, but about 4.30pm Edd paid me another visit for about fifteen minutes. He was alright, but very tired. He had not had more than a few hours sleep since the mutiny broke out. On Saturday afternoon he came again, this time to say that he was off for a five days trip to Kuala Lumpur to bring the German prisoners down from there. Mr Lowther Kemp and several of the Chinese Volunteers went with him. Edd said I was on no account to tell anyone where he was going. After they had left I was besieged with questions as to the movements of the little party. I finally said that I knew where they were going but was not allowed to say, and the nice folk left me alone after that, though some others still continued to worry me for a day or two. But never a word did they get out of me about the trip.

Saturday night I really went off to sleep properly for the first time since the mutiny. I felt Edd was quite safe, as he was on the sea. I must have been in a very heavy sleep, for at one o'clock Baba either called "Mummy" or cried out in her sleep, for I took one flying leap from the top berth where I was sleeping on to the floor, which was a most foolish thing to do. I badly strained my right ankle, and bruised my left arm and side rather severely, and felt all shaken up. Baba was fast asleep as I hobbled along to the pantry and woke up the boy, and made him give me a little Brandy which I soaked in a handkerchief and tied round my ankle, and then went back to bed again. But I hardly got any more sleep as my arm and ankle were aching very badly. In the morning folks noticed I was limping very much, so I had to say what I had done, and one lady kindly massaged my ankle for me, and did it a lot of good, and we tied it up as well as we could with handkerchiefs. The Captain insisted on rubbing it for me with some of his own patent lotion, and he nearly made me faint with the pain he gave me.

On Sunday we had a very nice service with Communion afterwards, and in the afternoon I went to sleep in the cabin. I did not mean to hurry as tea was not until 4.30, but at 3 o'clock there was such a noise going on, people walking about and launches hooting, that at last I gave up the idea of any more rest and began to dress, and Amah began to dress Baba. There seemed so much fuss that after a little while I called out to someone who was passing, to know if anything was the matter, and the good lady said we had to leave the ship. I said "I know we have to leave on Tuesday, but what is the use of getting in a fuss now?" She said "We have to leave at once". I waited to ask no more questions, but just flew into my clothes, finished dressing Baba, and sent her off with Amah to the Saloon to get some bread and jam, while I set to work to pack up the few things we had. The boy in the morning had brought me some clean clothes, and had taken away the bag he brought them in with the dirty ones, so I could not get half the things we had into the only small bag in my possession. But being a refugee this did not matter at all, I simply put a sheet on the floor and then threw everything on to it, tins of milk, hairbrush, shoes, sponge, toothbrushes and a piece of bread tied up in a handkerchief, bottle of Bovril, an orange, some sweets etc. It was a jumble, but in they all had to go. I then tied the corners together and as I had no string, I had to stick hairpins in to keep the sides together. I then went to the gangway with my little lot and stood there. I did not know what was the matter, or where we were going, but we evidently had to leave the *Ipoh* as three or four big launches were alongside.

I had not been standing there long before Mr Agnew came up to me and asked me if I knew why we were being turned off in such a hurry, and he told me that the ship was on fire! One of the coal bunkers was smouldering and it might burst into flame at any moment! He also told me to stay where I was until he came along with his wife and baby and he could take me in his launch to the Russian Cruiser which was lying still further out to sea.

We got away almost immediately. (I had dressed,

packed, and got ready in 15 minutes! One learns to be quick in wartime, even in a tropical climate.) We had a run of ten minutes in the launch to the Russian ship and had a very rough time getting there. Poor Baba cried all the time, I think she felt sick, and certainly frightened, but she soon got over it when we were off the launch and safely bestowed on the ship, which was an auxiliary cruiser, in peace time one of the Railway Steamers connecting Japan with the Siberian Railway. Our experiences on this ship must be left until another chapter.

Prince Eric of Denmark

Mary Brown

Our experiences on the Russian Ship were many and varied.
Only one of the officers knew English, and he hardly any at
all, so it was difficult to make people understand, but they
were most kind in every way and did all they could to make
us comfortable. But – oh dear – shall I ever forget the heat
of the ship! It was built for a cold climate, and there was
no passage of air through it anywhere. The Cabins were
large, but had tiny round portholes and no fans. We shared
a cabin with Mrs Swindell but as she slept on deck we saw
little of her. I was afraid to take Baba up on deck to sleep so
I stayed in the cabin with her, but it took me all my time not
to get hysterical in the cabin that first night. It was terribly
close and hot and in the middle of the night the electric light
went out, and it seemed absolutely stifling in the dark. I got
out of my berth and went to the door, but the passage was
hotter than the cabin. There was just a wee breeze coming
through the porthole, so I stayed there for a time, and in a

little while the lights came on again.

We were not allowed to have a bath before 8 o'clock in the morning, as the Officers wanted the bathrooms up to that time. I think this was the hardest thing of all; after a hot sticky night one felt one could not dress without bathing first.

Everything just at first was confusion; there were no chairs for us, so we sat on the floor. Mattresses had to be got, and blankets, before night-time, and these were brought from the Drill hall, and a large part of the deck was screened off for a bedroom and nearly everyone slept up there. I dared not leave Baba alone with Amah, as she had not got used to her again and did not understand what she said. I was glad afterwards that I had stayed down below and also that I had not been given a blanket, for a collection of 'livestock' came on board with the mattresses, and made the most of their time during the nights that followed, to the great discomfort of the ladies on deck! I never met one, I'm thankful to say!!

Each day on this boat was much the same as on the previous one; Ed came back on the Tuesday, and after a day or two on the *Klang* was put on to the staff at Government House, and I saw practically nothing of him as he could not get away. He tried to arrange with Miss Able to take us in as paying guests at the CEZMS school, on Government Hill, quite near to him. He had heard that a German Cruiser was supposed to be about, and he did not like us on the sea. This was on the Saturday, and he said I must go up to the school on Sunday morning if possible. However Miss Able came to see me and said she thought some of the children had whooping cough, and did not seem very keen on our going, so I asked her if she would see Ed, and arrange matters and let me know. She did not know about the German Cruiser, neither did other folks, and I couldn't say anything. Ed had to translate the private telegram about it, and that is how he knew. I did not feel nervous, as I knew Ed would hear anything there was to know and would get us out of danger if there was any.

By this time several ladies had gone to their houses, but our house and several others were still in the danger zone, so we could not go back. There were quite a number of us, and about thirteen children, left on Sunday, and several ladies said to me "You stay on board, you are better here". I said, "So many people are leaving I don't want to stay on board, as I don't want to be the last, and I can't get at my husband very well now, he is so busy". This good lady, who was at the head of affairs on board, and who lives quite near us, said, "I am going to stay until the very last, so you will be quite all right while I am here and besides there is no hurry for us to leave this ship." So I sent Ed a chit and told him what this lady had said, and added that I would rather stay where I was until I could get back to our house again. Our house would be considered in the 'safe' area by Monday.

At tiffin time on Monday we all seemed to be on board, and there was no talk of people leaving, and Mrs Pears and I had a rest on deck after tiffin, and just about tea-time we were puzzling over the sock that I was making for the Tommies at home, when it began to dawn upon us that there were very few people about. We went to our cabins to tidy up for tea, and just as I got to the Saloon I saw the lady with whom I had had the conversation the day before with her hat on, evidently going ashore! I didn't think anything about it, and she asked me to find another lady and tell her that they were ready and waiting for her, which I did, and I thought they were just going for a run on shore for an hour or so. I went up to see them off, and there heard a remark which made me prick up my ears, and I asked one of the people if they were coming back, and she said, "No, nearly everyone has left this afternoon." This lady immediately began to go down the gangway, and I shouted to her to ring up my husband and ask him what I was to do. I had had a chit from Ed to say he could not get away on Monday at all but if I could get ashore he could meet me at 6 o'clock at the Club on Tuesday evening, and we could have a chat.

I immediately found Mrs Pears and told her what was going on, and we both came up on deck only to find that the launch had left. Mr Pears was busy and could not get away until late on Tuesday, so we two were in rather a hole, and we heard quite casually that everyone had to be off the ship by 1pm the next day.

We felt furiously angry at the way we had been treated, the very people who had told me to stay had just slipped away and said nothing at all to me about going. Mrs Pears had a little girl about 7 months old, and I had Barbara, and we each had an Amah. There was no other launch out to the ship or one to the shore, so we could do nothing. That night there were just six ladies, our two children, and two Amahs left on board. It was not very nice to be there left alone with all the Russian crew and officers, but we made the best of it. I hoped the lady would remember to ring up Hubby. I also asked her to ring up my 'Boy' as well, and tell him to come early next morning. Fortunately for me she did this.

Our last night was most exciting. Prince Eric of Denmark came on board to dine with the Captain and Officers. After dinner I went to the cabin to see if Baba was asleep, and while I was gone one of the Officers invited the ladies on to the upper deck to watch some Russian dancing. When I came on deck I could not see anyone about. I walked round and round and then met one of the sailors, who pointed to the upper deck. But I did not like to go up, I did not know that the rest of the ladies were there, and then one of the officers came for me, so up I went, and as I walked across the deck to where the ladies were sitting there was dead silence, and then everybody, the Prince included, laughed and laughed. It appeared that they thought I was going to dance or sing! The dancing was not very exciting; once or twice one of the officers dressed up in a sheepskin which smelt as if it had never been dressed; I was nearly sick; the officer near me upset me very much by telling me it was a 'mutton skin', but with great presence of mind I managed not to laugh.

At about 10.30 we got away, and Mrs Pears and I went to our cabins and began to prepare for bed, when we heard a waltz tune being played in the Dining Room, and on looking out through our cabin door down the passage we saw the ladies dancing with the officers. They kept it up until quite late and got very lively. I felt very much inclined to shut and lock my cabin door, but could not stand the heat, so pulled the curtain across as usual and hoped I should not be disturbed. Amah slept in the cabin with me and Mrs Pears, Amah and Baba were in the cabin next to me, but no-one else was down below; the others were sleeping on deck.

I had quite a good night and was up at 6am and did my packing, as I did not know what was before me at all. It was a good thing I did it, for Rev Mr Peile came off in a launch for me at 8.30. Edd had rung him up and asked him to come out with a note for me, and to get me ashore. Our 'Boy' also arrived. He finished my packing for me, and then helped Mrs Pears with hers. Mr Peile kindly waited while we ate a little breakfast. Then we wished the Captain Goodbye and thanked him for his kindness etc and off we set. Edd's note said I had better go up to Government House and see him and arrange what to do. Mrs Pears also did not know what to do, so I took her to the Club and rang up her Hubby, and he managed to get off and come down to her. Ed had rung up the syce to meet me with the carriage, so when we arrived at Johnston's Pier I sent the boy home with the luggage in a gharry, and Baba and I drove up to Government House. I had made up my mind that if it was safe I would go home, and Ed assured me that it was absolutely safe. The General himself came out and very kindly added his assurances to Ed's, and said I need not be at all afraid as there were picquets out all round our neighbourhood, but he would arrange for a special one quite near our house. I did not stay long at Headquarters, as Ed was very busy, and he said he would come up about 6pm and see how we were getting on.

It felt strange driving along the Roads on our way home, and it was hard to realize that there had been fighting going on, everything looked so peaceful, and our house as fresh and neat as a new pin. The boys had been splendid, nothing had been stolen, and the house and beds and even my frocks and shoes etc had been aired and kept nice. I had half expected to find my dresses and shoes mouldy. I don't know why, but I did not feel at all nervous really.

Ed came up at 6 o'clock and had a bath and a change of clothes, and we had a wee chat and then off he went at 6.30, and he did this most days for a fortnight. At about 8 o'clock that night Ed rang me up to say that the General had told him that he did not want him, and that he was to go home and stay with his wife, that she would probably be a little nervous. This was very kind of him, for he did Ed's work himself that night. I was more than pleased; he did not arrive until about 11pm and was dead fagged, but had quite a good sleep and was about again next morning at 5.45am.

I was alone in the house for two weeks. A good many people kindly asked us to stay with them until Ed could get home again, but I refused all the invitations for Baba's sake. I felt I must get the poor little girlie settled down at home; and get some nicely cooked food for her again; she was really rather upset through living on tinned mutton soup and chicken broth and other tinned things. We had had about five weeks on the boat coming out, then three days in the Hotel here, and less than a fortnight in our own house before the mutiny broke out, and then we had one week on the SS Ipoh and another in the Russian ship, so we were so thankful to be in our own house at last.

Nothing at all exciting happened during our first fortnight at home. I had really a very lonely time of it and I hardly saw a soul. Most of the people were still in the Hotels, or staying with their friends nearer town; two of the houses near us were still shut up.

Poor Baba could not understand why Daddy did not come. She kept saying "Why doesn't my Daddy come and play with me?" so many times, and quite fretted for him, and when he did come she just put her arms round his neck and Mummy couldn't get near at all, and we sometimes had tears when he went away.

I was very fortunate in having been one of the *Ipoh* crowd; we were the most comfortable of all the Refugees. The people on the SS *Nile*, which was the transport that was to have taken the 5th LI away, had a terrible time. A lot of lower class Eurasians were on board, and they literally fought for the food, and there did not seem to be enough water for washing or drinking purposes. But I must not tell here of the experiences of others. This is a personal narrative, and the lot of others, although very interesting, is not the object of this story.

Cleaning Up

Edwin A. Brown

I finished my last chapter with the remark that the first phase of the Mutiny had been dealt with. It is now necessary for the sake of clarity to say something about the cleaning-up process, so that this personal account of our experiences may be made complete.

Kemp and I, having had some tiffin at the Club, felt that we had better get back to the Drill Hall again. On arrival there we found that another batch of prisoners had been rounded up, and had been brought in from other parts of the island. There was no way of looking after them properly in the precincts of the Drill Hall, so an empty ship in the harbour was commandeered, and I was told off to take them to it and put them safely on board. My duties were to cease when I handed over the prisoners to the man on board. I thought that it would be a good thing if the people in the streets could see these men being marched off in custody, so I elected to take them on foot to Johnston's Pier under a strong guard. For this purpose I rounded up as many of the odds and ends of my Chinese as I could lay my hands on, as they, and they only, of the men at the Drill Hall had any knowledge of the meaning of discipline, told them to fix bayonets and surround the batch of prisoners, and then we marched off having arranged for government launches to await us at the Pier. I think that our procession did a good deal to calm the fears of the natives in the streets. I handed over the prisoners, and decided to take a few minutes French Leave and go and see my family. This I did, and the visit is reported upon in my wife's portion of this account.

Then we went back to the Drill Hall again for further orders. By this time darkness had fallen, and as before the streets were unlighted. I reported my return, and immediately got orders to proceed at once to Government House with a guard of forty men, as the Johore forces that were supposed to be on duty there had decided to return as a body to Johore Bahru, the official excuse being that they had to bury the man who had been shot at the prison camp the day before. The result was that Government House, now the Military Headquarters, was without any means of defence whatsoever. Again I had to gather odds and ends, my own men being required again by Glennie for his Drill Hall Guard during the night, and after picking forty or so, and taking Kemp along with me, this time as my official second in command, we climbed into lorries once more and set off in the dark for Government House. I think I should just mention here that the refusal of Major Glennie to let me have my own men was understandable. He had been my predecessor in command of the Chinese company and, like me, had complete trust in them, and it is quite understandable that he should want to keep at least one portion of his little force by his side for use in any emergency that might arise. So I had to be content with my 'dug-ups' once more.

On arriving at Government House we found all in darkness, no men to be seen, and a very large consignment of Tins of Motor Spirit lying out in the open alongside the building. I set off in search of the General, and in going round found my way into that part of the building that houses the Governor's private offices. All doors were wide open, so I walked in, to find myself in the presence of Sir Arthur Young, the Governor, and Sir George Maxwell, the head in the Native States, who had come down to Singapore to be with the Governor on the spot. I addressed myself without warning to Sir Arthur, and said that he should have his doors shut, it was unsafe to leave them open. My voice, coming out of the darkness as it did, gave them an awful shock, which in Maxwell's case resulted in his slipping on the polished floor and falling backwards into the waste paper basket, from which Sir Arthur and myself had to extricate him. Explanations as to my presence followed, the General was found, and I learned that I was to be in complete charge of the military arrangements in the precincts and was to take what measures I felt necessary for the defence of the house in case of need. The first thing I did was to order the Governor to shut all his doors. Then I went back to my men and sought a place for the safe disposal of the Petrol which was very dangerously situated at the moment, as a bullet into a tin might set the whole consignment off. I had my men cart all the tins into the upper drawing room of the house where it would be free from the sight of a snooper, though I felt some qualms at putting the tins on the nice big carpet. However, it was the only place at the moment, as the absence of any light made looking for other suitable places impossible.

The next thing was to establish guards and posts, a difficult matter under the circumstances, as not many of my men understood what they had to do, and duties had to be explained over and over again to each individual. Everything at the new headquarters was at sixes and sevens. It had been decided the day before to move HQ from Fort Canning to Government House, but all the Military Staff had been ordered to 'the Field' and means of removing were reduced to a minimum. The only officer left at Fort Canning was a

Major named Spriggs, up till just lately a civilian attached to the RE Services for the care of buildings and such like. These had lately been put into uniform and granted military rank, for the sake of better order and discipline. But of course they had no military training or experience, and so it was that, when the Mutiny broke out, and it was a question of 'all hands to the pumps', poor Major Spriggs was left on his lonesome at Fort Canning and forgotten. He decided that he was worse than useless where he was, so he packed up all important papers and files, and got a relay of rickshaws and moved the whole stock to Government House, looking for some safe place. There he found the General (Col Ridout had received a cable promoting him to Brigadier General on the night the Mutiny broke out) but no Staff of any description, and so he was turned into chief Factotum until things could be organized a little. I knew him well, he was a faithful member of the Cathedral Choir, and a sound and sensible man. So naturally I turned to him with my problems, and we did what we could to get things into some sort of order.

I got hold of the General after a time, and put my difficulties before him, and suggested that I should be allowed to get in touch with the Drill Hall and get my own men, the Chinese Company, to replace the odds and ends that we were dealing with, and he thought it a good plan and directed that I should deal with it as soon as the daylight came. Then I thought it was about time I had a bit of rest, but this alas was not to be, for the General carried me off to a little room he was using as an office, and told me I should have to deal with all telegrams from the War Office and other places, as he had absolutely no-one to do the work. So thereupon he initiated me into the secret code in use at the time for official messages, and I sat down to master the thing. Now the War Office telegrams began to come in soon after 10pm, so I handed over to Kemp the duties with the guard, and got down to my new job. I was not used to it, and was therefore slow, and dawn was breaking before I finished for the night. So rest was impossible for another long period.

As soon as possible I got onto the Drill Hall, and found that my whole Company had returned from their duties at Blakan Mati, and so were available for work elsewhere. I told Glennie, still in charge at the Drill Hall, of the new orders about the Government House guard, and he promised to send me the required thirty men as soon as possible. Then I got on to Lieut Song Ong Siang, my second in command, and told him to arrange for the regular sending of rations for our men, fixed that up, and then thought about some food for myself. There was none to be had, no arrangements had been thought of for feeding any of the troops, and I came across Major Spriggs hunting around in the back premises of Government House, looking for something that might be called breakfast. Appeals to the gentleman who called himself 'Major Domo' proving of no use – he either could not or would not provide us with anything – we eventually sat down at a little serving table outside the door of the Governor's breakfast room, and waited until any plate or dish was brought out by the boys, when we immediately grabbed the remains of the food, and managed with that. I may say here that nothing was done to feed us at all for the rest of the week, and we subsisted for meals in this manner until one day we were so hungry that we cut into a very nice looking and succulent boiled ham, and did ourselves well on that. It turned out that the Governor also was very partial to boiled ham, and liked to carve it himself. The joint in question, contrary to what we thought, had not been brought out but was waiting to be carried in to the Gubernatorial breakfast table, and the balloon in consequence went up. But the row did good, for, soon after, the Officers of the Staff were given a room to themselves for meals and arrangements were made for proper food to be supplied and cooked.

However, this morning, the Wednesday after the Mutiny, other things were happening. The new Guard turned up, and I was very glad to see them and to find them in charge of my two best Sergeants, Liang Quee and Chow Kim, both old soldiers and very reliable men. As soon as they were settled in and the necessary guard posted, I was visited by these two Sergeants who brought me the rumour, which they assured me they knew to be true, that Diehn, the escaped German head of Behn Meyer and Co, who had been in the POW camp at Tanglin, had walked out when the rest of the prisoners escaped, and made his way to his house in Grange Road, where he had had a bath, changed his clothes, and gone down to the house of his second store keeper near the Municipal Store, where he had spent the night. I was assured that, if they could get away at once with a detachment of men, there was every possibility of Diehn being captured. Whatever truth there was in this news, I thought it advisable to acquaint the General at once, and ask permission to go and find whether it was true or not. Then started my first experience of the ineptitude of the powers that were in charge at the time. The General said that the matter was one for the Police. On being rung up, the IGP [Inspector General of Police] said that he had no men available and that in any case it was a matter for the Military. Arguments ensued, and about noon the IGP came up himself to Government House to discuss the matter. I was of course fuming; whether the rumour was true or not, it should have been dealt with without any delay. At last, after a long wait, I got orders to send off a search party – at three o'clock in the afternoon. Of course there was no Diehn to be found, and actually at this time he was away to sea with the other escapees, but my men have always insisted that if they could have gone when they reported the matter they would have caught Diehn, and knowing the way the Chinese have of getting news about among themselves, I still think that the rumour they brought me was true.

However there was no help for it, and the matter had to be forgotten.

By now there was appearing some semblance of order about Headquarters. Major Watson had come back from his duties at the P&O Wharf, and had been installed as "A" (which in civilian language means DAAG [Deputy Assistant Adjutant General] and QMG [Quartermaster General]) and young Lieut Oliver, who had been with Brownlow in the field, was taken on as GSO1 [General Staff Officer (Grade 1)]. I was made GSO2 (acting) and Kemp was put in as assistant to Watson. Our positions were in addition to our other duties. I had to go out in the morning at times as Liaison Officer with the troops in the field, and deal with all cable messages at night and all the odds and ends of jobs that were found to be necessary, so I handed over to Kemp the actual duties of the Guard.

It was about this time too that some primitive

arrangements were thought of for making the life of the staff at least possible. Some mattresses were brought in and laid down on the floor of the Ballroom, and the far portion of the room opposite the entrance was screened off as an office for the 'highs'. On these mattresses the Staff was supposed to take its evening sleep, but as far as I was concerned rest and sleep of an evening was just one of those things that one dreams about but never actually experiences, for after a day's work which consisted, among other things, of going out into the Operation Field carrying orders and instructions to the numerous troops and sailors of various nationalities that were by now pouring in to our aid, and generally acting as Liaison Officer, I had my evenings fully occupied with the Cable work, which took me the greater part of the night to cope with. I calculated at the time that in the first seven days of this strenuous time I actually lay down only for eleven hours.

On this Wednesday afternoon the General came to me and asked me if I thought I could find a way of providing a small ship with enough food to enable it to go to sea for a few days. He wanted to send some men to sea to provide a patrol to stop mutineers from escaping from the island to the mainland. This was a poser, as of course all shops were still closed and no transport of any kind was to be seen in the streets. However it was obvious that something must be done, so I said I would try and oblige. I remembered that there was a fairly prosperous provision dealers in Orchard Road at the bottom of Cavanagh Road and I thought that I might find a jaga or coolie of some sort on the premises, so I got a lorry from our stock of transport, took some men with me, and set off to see what I could do. Arriving at the shop, I was lucky in finding a coolie there, so giving him a note to give the management when they came back, I proceeded to break into the place, and loaded up my lorry with anything I could find that I thought might provide means of sustenance for about twenty men for some days. It was all guess work of course, and I am afraid that the provision of regular or ordered meals was out of the question, but I 'stole' tins of cooked ham, tins of bully beef, sacks of potatoes and rice, cases of tinned biscuits, supplies of tea coffee and sugar, and when I thought that I had sufficient I loaded up my lorry with the loot and my men, and set off for Johnston's Pier, quite well satisfied with myself. When I got to the pier I found the General there, and near by a small steamer that he had commandeered for his needs. He told me that he had collected a score of suitable men from his few forces in the field, and had ordered them in to rendezvous at the pier, and wanted a meal for them before they went on board. This was a real poser, but I suggested that with his permission I might be able to do something about the matter with the

Singapore Club, and accordingly went over and put the case to Bill Mayson, the Secretary. He agreed to put his cooks on the job at once, and so, when the dirty and disreputable twenty turned up from the outfield, they found themselves provided with a slap-up Club dinner, reinforced by various 'extras' provided by several generous members of the Club who happened to be on the premises. In the meantime I had loaded my provisions on to the steamer, and in due course saw the expedition sail off on its lawful occasions, with most of its personnel contentedly smoking big fat cigars. I never heard any more about the matter, or whether any good came of the expedition, but the matter was brought to my attention several months later by a nice old gentleman up at Fort Canning who rang me up and said he had received some bills from the Singapore Club which he had been asked to pay, and that he couldn't find anything in Army Regulations which warranted troops being provided with cigars. I referred him to the general and left it at that.

About this time our strength was increased by the advent of some members of a new force called, for want of a better name, the Home Guard. They consisted of the more elderly members of the community that had been roped in to take over duties more suitable to their age than actual field work, and they were sent up to me to make use of in patrolling the grounds of Government House. I gave them the Guard Room for their Headquarters, and in the course of the evening went round to see how they were getting on. They were armed with any kind of weapon that had been found for them, at a time when Army rifles were very difficult to obtain. Old 'Tower of London' shotguns seemed to be in the majority, but there were some Lee Metfords, and to my horror I found one bright old gentleman busily employed in trying to hammer in, with the butt end of a bayonet, a 'Tower of London' cartridge into the breech of a Lee Metford 303. I hesitate to think what might have happened if he had hit hard enough.

The next day the General got hold of me and suggested a bath. It must be remembered that it was now Thursday, and with the exception of a tub at the Club after the morning's work at Alexandra, I had had no opportunity for cleansing operations of any sort, and I had been getting wet through with perspiration several times a day. I had no clothes to change into, but I took the offer with thankfulness, and remember being much amused at the antediluvian kind of bathroom I was given for use, with its built in brick bath. However I felt a bit cleaner when I had washed.

On Saturday morning the General came to me and confided that he had received an urgent call from Kuala Lumpur that the Authorities there were getting the wind up concerning the large force of Sikh Police in the Native

States, and asking him to relieve them of the necessity of taking charge of the forty or fifty German internees that had been sent to Kuala Lumpur for safekeeping. He had decided to bring the batch to Singapore, and wanted me to go up at once and bring them down. He said that he would try and find an adequate guard for me to take with me, but I said he needn't worry; if I had to go I would take my own reliable Chinese as a guard, to which he agreed. This meant a sea journey, as there was no railway through at the time. So I set off at once for the Singapore Club, after ringing up the Straits Steamship and finding that the manager was over there having tiffin. I got hold of Harold Somerville and asked him to keep the afternoon steamer back until I could get on board, and to order into Port Swettenham another steamer from Penang that could be got into the port by the Monday afternoon. Then, these arrangements having been completed, I pushed off back to Government House to collect my men and get my final orders from the General. I got hold of Kemp and told him to get ready to come with me, picked the two Sergeants already referred to and twelve men, and was ready to start by about 4.30pm.

The first thing to be done was to try and get some clothes. It must be remembered that all this time we had been living in a pair of khaki shorts and a shirt, with no change of clothes whatsoever and with only two baths to our credit, and we could not possibly go to Kuala Lumpur in the condition we were in. So, sending the men on to Johnston's Pier in a lorry, we grabbed a car and four men with loaded rifles and set off for my house to see what we could do in the matter. We had to take a guard with us, as we had no knowledge of the condition of things in the suburbs. Singapore was being gradually cleaned up, but the cleared zone had not as yet got further than the junction of Orchard and Grange Road, and my house was at the Tanglin Road end of Grange Road. No excitement however occurred on our way, and we arrived at my house to find the kebun mowing the lawn and the house bedding out on the verandah in the usual way for airing purposes. Everything looked strangely peaceful and home-like. My Chinese boy, James, was busy in the house and I soon got him to work packing bags for both of us – my clothes being fortunately a good fit for Kemp also. James told me that the mutineers had been all over the house and garden within half an hour of my wife's leaving the place, but since then there had been no disturbance to mar the day's peace.

Leaving word with him to go to the ship with a replenishment of clothes for the 'Mem', we got in our car and pushed off to the Pier, where we collected our men and a Government Launch and went off to the Straits Steamship boat which was waiting for our arrival as ordered. On the way I paid a visit to my wife on the SS *Ipoh* but warned her not to say anything to anybody about where we were bound for. We caused a considerable flutter on arrival at the *Ipoh* and again when we got to our own steamer, but that was understandable. It was dinner time when we got on board, so Kemp and I decided to feed at once, as it would be the first sit-down meal we had had for a week. Alas, it was not to be. Before we had got past the soup stage we noticed that the passengers were sniffing the air, and then one or two got up and left the saloon. We began to wonder, and it suddenly dawned on our horrified minds that we ourselves were the cause of the commotion. We smelt!! So we left hurriedly, had the rest of our food brought up on deck, and as soon as we had eaten went down to the bathrooms, and had our first decent clean-up for a week. The joy of it!!! We were clean again at last. Both of us went straight to bed after our baths, and slept until we were tying up at Port Swettenham. Our men too seemed to have benefited from their quiet night on board, and altogether we looked very smart and warlike as we marched onto the station platform to the waiting train. The arrival of our men caused the intensest excitement among the people on the station and the passengers on the train. There were several ladies among them, and anyone who could claim the slightest acquaintance with either Kemp or myself tried their best to pump us, but without success. We arrived at Kuala Lumpur on time and were there met by senior police officers, causing more surprise and speculation. The necessity for secrecy was paramount, as of course the suspicions of the authorities as to the faithlessness of the native police could not be made known, and nothing could be said about the German internees until they had all been rounded up and collected. I was soon closeted with the IGP in his office, and it was arranged that we should board the train back to Port Swettenham after tiffin on the Monday, and that the police would be responsible for bringing everyone concerned to the platform of departure for me to take over charge.

In due course we found ourselves at the station on the Monday, gazing at a mountain of household furniture from dining tables to double beds and mirrored dressing tables, and at the sixty-five owners of the same. I told the police that I would take the Germans, but that they could be responsible for sending the impedimenta down to Singapore after us, and to this they had to agree, but I fear with a bad grace. The prisoners were very much upset when I allowed them only such 'personal effects' luggage as they could carry in their own hands, which they would have to do from the train to the ship, but finally I got them all into line, checked them with the police lists, told them off to the various carriages, disposed my guard strategically with instructions to jump off the train and watch both sides at any stoppage on the way, gave a clean receipt for the 'cargo' to the Kuala Lumpur police, and finally steamed away on our journey back to Singapore.

I had been told by the Kuala Lumpur authorities that while the majority of the people were respectable German merchants of Singapore and Penang, there were a few young rubber planters and miners of a questionable spirit, and I therefore took care that they should be specially watched.

We got safely on board, and sailed. As soon as we had got away I visited the Captain and explained the position to him. It must be remembered that his only knowledge was contained in a telegram to him before he left Penang, ordering him to put into Port Swettenham 'for orders', and he was considerably surprised to find what those 'orders' consisted of. The boat was only a small one, and as a rule did not carry many passengers, though it had the usual number of cabins. The Captain told me that the trouble was water, and that his stock would not be enough to enable him to cater for so many people. So making the best of a bad job, I told him that I would allow free to each prisoner one bottled drink at each meal other than breakfast, and with this concession he thought that he could manage the water situation. It is I think advisable here to mention one of the conditions of my position, namely that I was in no circumstances to treat the internees as prisoners of war, but as members of the public kept together for security reasons through no fault of their own, and General Ridout had stressed this point very emphatically. As a matter of fact the majority of my prisoners were well known to me, and many occupied or had occupied important positions in the business and social world of the Colony. The few unknown quantities, the up-country planters and the miners, were not sufficiently large in numbers to cause any inconvenience, and the few 'ladies of easy virtue' who had been deported by the Kuala Lumpur authorities behaved themselves after I had locked them in their cabins for one night to show them that they weren't on a pleasure cruise.

When we arrived in Singapore Harbour I told the Captain not to go alongside, but to anchor somewhere in the roads until I could find out what was going to happen to us. As soon as we had dropped anchor I went ashore and took a conveyance to Government House to see what was to happen. I found that no arrangements – other than talk – had been made for us, and the end of it was that I was told to keep my people on board the ship for the present; so back I went to my charge. We had anchored within sight of the Russian Cruiser, to which I paid a visit as soon as I got settled down on my ship, for I had found out about the fire on the SS *Ipoh*, and the consequent transference of thee refugees to the warship in question.

Then I settled down to a rather weary wait, with no chance of any excitement and very little to do outside regular guard duties. This went on for about a week, when orders came to hand over my charge to a new guard and commander, and to return to Headquarters complete with my men.

We were glad to get back again, and to find when we resumed our duties that living was very much easier. Though our beds were still only mattresses on the ballroom floor, a special room with an electric fan had been given us for meals and there was regular service. The only trouble was that the room contained the favourite cockatoo of the Lady Evelyn Young, the Governor's wife. So much did this bird trouble us that I decided one morning to cover its cage up with one of the rugs on the floor. Thereupon peace ensued, until Lady Evelyn collared me one morning after breakfast, and held forth at some considerable length upon the ungentlemanly behaviour of someone unknown who had dared to be so rude as to deal with her pet parrot in so dastardly a manner. I think she left me eventually perfectly sure that whatever specimen of the rough genus known as British Officer was responsible for the outrage, it could not possibly have been me.

By this time Singapore was full of armed forces, and it

was obvious that the Mutiny, as a time of emergency, was drawing to an end. The sphere of safety in the town was being enlarged, and there came a day when the General came to me and said that the only lady left on the ships who had no husband to look after her on shore was my wife. He had decided therefore to bring her home, and suggested that she should come up to Headquarters on her way, and he would provide an adequate guard on our house during the day and night so that she should not feel nervous. I too wanted to get her off the Russian ship, where she was very uncomfortable, so she was brought along with Amah and Barbara to Government House, where the General welcomed her and explained the position. That evening about seven o'clock, he came to me and suggested that a night's holiday would do me good, and ordered me to go home to my wife for the night. This was a very kind thought on his part, especially as he offered to do my cable work himself. He was rewarded by being able to translate the War Office telegram that night announcing his own promotion to Major General.

It was now becoming apparent that things would soon be back at normal again. Troops that had come to our aid were being reviewed by the Governor preparatory to leaving us, and at length Headquarters went back to Fort Canning, and I announced my intention of going back again to my office.

And so came to an end the Singapore Mutiny of 1915. Looking back, I am of the opinion that two little things saved Singapore from disaster on the fateful day. One thing was the action of Admiral Jerram who, when he first heard of the outbreak, posted off full speed to the little 'Cadmus' which was lying alongside the Dock wharf with most of her engines on the dock, and ordered every man on board from the Captain to the Cabin boy to arm themselves immediately and to push off along the road to Pasir Panjang, and to shoot to kill any Indian who they met with a rifle in his hands. It was found out afterwards that through this prompt order the real ringleader of the Mutineers was killed.

The other thing was Singapore's luck in having a man like Col Brownlow in command of the operations in the field, instead of a 'theoretical soldier' who alas comprised the majority of officers in those early days of the 1914 War, who would have followed orders, and so given the mutineers time to consolidate and to march on Singapore at their leisure.

Yes, I think we could count ourselves lucky.

Postscript

Edwin A. Brown

There would seem to be some slight necessity of explaining some little matters that have been left 'in the air' in the narrative.

First of all, therefore, I think it is necessary to explain the position of our family at the time this story opens.

It will be wondered, perhaps, why an active officer in the Volunteers should be 'unattached' at a time when the country and Empire was at war. We had only been back in the Colony from long leave for a few days when the Mutiny broke out. Chinese New Year coincided with our arrival, and it was my intention to report officially my return as soon as those holidays were over. We had gone on leave in the spring of 1914, and the World War broke out before that leave was over. I had in my possession letters from Officialdom in Singapore showing that I had passed the territorial examination for Field Officer, and suggesting that facilities might be given me for some more advanced experience in Military matters than was possible in Singapore, but I had not presented these to the War Office when war broke out, and then it was too late. A serious talk with my wife resulted in a decision to offer myself for active service, and an extension of leave to enable me to do so was obtained from my Firm.

I was, however, just over the age for service, as it stood at the time, and though I tried hard, even to paying personal visits to the War Office, and enlisting the help of Sir John Anderson, the Permanent Under Secretary of State for the Colonies, who had just been promoted to his position from the Governorship of Singapore, and who was a personal friend of mine and who knew all about me, but I was unsuccessful in getting taken on, and so, my extension of leave having expired, I had to return to Singapore, and, as I have said, arrived back just in time to be on the spot when the Mutiny broke out.

Another matter that wants a bit of clarifying is the discrepancy that may be noticed between this account of the happenings and the official report as published in the despatches.

I have, earlier in this narrative, referred to the message that was handed to me on the Wharf by Major Watson, to take down to Col Brownlow at the advanced base. At the time I wrote that portion of this account, I thought it politic to curtail the wording of that message somewhat, as the happenings were too recent for safety. Now that I am finishing my little history, however, some time later, I think that there can be no harm in giving the message in full. The important words, now put on paper for the first time, were that Col Brownlow was advised to retire from his advanced position, and to take up an 'interior' position on the foothills surrounding the General Hospital and the Gaol.

When I delivered this written document to Brownlow at the corner of Alexandra Road and Pasir Panjang Road, as already recorded, and after he had read it, he handed the message to me. He gave me a chance to read it again, looked at me, and said "Brown, you have never seen this message, have you?", and I, feeling that there was something funny about his remark, and guessing what was toward, said promptly "No, sir." Brownlow then quietly and deliberately tore up the paper, held it in the flame of the little lamp till it had burnt away, and said, "That is over then, we shall attack from here as soon as it is light enough."

I suspect that previous instructions from Headquarters were more in accordance with his own ideas than these later timid ones that I had brought down to him, and he didn't want it known that such orders had been received by him. Of course his decision was the right one, even I could see the danger of retiring now when we had the advantage of surprise on our side.

Finally, there is the point of difference between what is officially reported in the despatch, and the actual happenings at Alexandra immediately the operations there were over. But it must be remembered that I have put down in this account the things that actually happened, without any reference to diplomatic 'second thoughts'. And bearing in mind the 'wigging' that certain senior Officers received from the peppery tongue of a disappointed Commander, the 'Official' report, when it appeared in the papers, caused me great amusement.

I found out afterwards that Col Ridout and Col Brownlow were actually commissioned into the army at the same time almost to a day, that Brownlow had almost continual active service in war to his credit, while Ridout's war service was mainly behind the lines in the South African War, and it is probable that he had never seen a shot fired in anger, and certainly had no practical experience of the situation that we were experiencing. Brownlow, on the contrary, knew the Indian mentality thoroughly, and therefore was far more competent to make a decision on the matter at hand than Ridout could possibly hope to be.

Also by Edwin A. Brown

INDISCREET MEMORIES
1901 SINGAPORE THROUGH THE EYES
OF A COLONIAL ENGLISHMAN

Stepping off the SS *Hamburg* on a moonlit night in January 1901, Edwin A. Brown knew little about his new home, the Straits Settlement of Singapore. Through diary extracts and personal memories, this young Englishman brings to life characters and events in a country few would recognise today.

Life for the early settlers was always eventful. Entertainment came in the form of comic operas, visiting circuses, balls at Government House and socialising at the Tingel Tangel dance hall. There were rickshaw strikes, sightings of a sea serpent in the Singapore harbour, Sunday morning horse rides around the Settlement and tigers causing havoc in Chinatown.

From the death of Queen Victoria and the coronation of King Edward to the decision by Straits-born Chinese to discard their *towchang* (queues), we come to understand how historical events shaped and affected the society of the day.